GOD LOVES HER

FOR GIRLS

GOD LOVES HER

90 FAITH-BUILDING DEVOTIONS

Our Daily Bread
Publishing.

Requests for permission to quote from this book should be directed to: Permissions Department, Our Daily Bread Publishing, PO Box 3566, Grand Rapids, MI 49501, or contact us by email at permissionsdept@odb.org.

Interior design by Patti Brinks

Library of Congress Cataloging-in-Publication Data

Names: Our Daily Bread (Organization), contributor.
Title: God loves her for girls : 90 faith-building devotions / Our Daily Bread.
Description: Grand Rapids, MI : Our Daily Bread Publishing, 2024. | Audience:
    Ages 8-12 | Summary: "In 90 devotions that dig into the Bible each day, girls 8
    to 12 will learn that God created them for a purpose, loves them, and cares about
    every detail of their lives" -- Provided by publisher.
Identifiers: LCCN 2023054278 (print) | LCCN 2023054279 (ebook) | ISBN
    9781640703308 (paperback) | ISBN 9781640703315 (epub)
Subjects: LCSH: Girls--Prayers and devotions--Juvenile literature.
Classification: LCC BV4860 .G646 2024 (print) | LCC BV4860 (ebook) | DDC
    242/.62--dc23/eng/20240125
LC record available at https://lccn.loc.gov/2023054278
LC ebook record available at https://lccn.loc.gov/2023054279

Printed in the United States of America
24 25 26 27 28 29 30 31 / 8 7 6 5 4 3 2 1

INTRODUCTION

Every girl needs to know she's loved. And you know what? You are. You're loved by the Creator of the universe! God loves you so much that He created the world for your care and your enjoyment.

Even better than that, He sent His Son to die for you so you could be with Him forever. You probably know the verse: "For God so loved the world that he gave his one and only Son, that whoever believes in him shall not perish but have eternal life." That's John 3:16. God loves you. All that God wants in return is that you love Him too.

The devotional stories in this book encourage you to do three things. First, know you are loved. Second, get to know more about God. And third, learn to love and live for Him.

You've got your whole life ahead of you. Now is the best time to begin making great choices. The best choice ever is to choose God.

Open these pages and dig in. God loves you.

DEPTHS OF LOVE

See what great love the Father has lavished on us, that we should be called children of God! And that is what we are!

1 JOHN 3:1

Three-year-old Dylan McCoy had just learned to swim when he fell through a rotted plywood covering into a forty-foot deep, stone-walled well in his grand-father's backyard. Dylan managed to stay afloat in ten feet of water until he was rescued. Although firefighters brought ropes to raise the boy, the father was so worried about his son that he climbed down the slippery rocks to help him to safety.

Most parents would do anything for their children!

When the apostle John wrote to first-century believers who were struggling to be courageous, he encouraged them with these words: "See what great love the Father has lavished on us, that we should be called children of God! And that is what we are!" (1 John 3:1).

If you believe in God, He calls you His child! Just as there are actions a parent will take only for their child—like Dylan's dad climbing into a well to save him—God went to great lengths to rescue His children. He sent His only Son to die for our sins. If you haven't already, you can ask Him into your heart today.

Do you need God to rescue you?

Jesus, thank you for loving me so much that you died for me.

You can read about how much Father
God loves you in 1 John 3:1–6.

DAY 2

GOD KNOWS YOUR STORY

Search me, God, and know my heart;
test me and know my anxious thoughts.

PSALM 139:23

It's great to have a best friend! You and your friend have fun playing and hanging out together—whether that's shooting hoops, making jewelry, or watching movies—but you also talk about important things. You can even tell her your secrets. Sometimes you argue or disagree about what you want to do, but you always work it out.

But now and then, there's something you don't want to or can't talk to your friend about. It's too embarrassing. And you don't think your parents would understand. You don't know who to tell about your feelings.

There's someone you can talk to about anything. And that's God! When you pray, you're talking to Him. He hears and understands. If you're confused or worried or sad, you can tell Him. He loves you and wants to help. If you're sorry about something you did, He forgives you

when you ask. Just as you enjoy talking to your friend, He loves it when you pray. He knows all about you, and He wants you to get to know and love Him too. You do that by reading the Bible. It tells you all about Him.

What do you want to talk to God about right now?

God, I'm so glad I can talk to you about anything.
Help me to pray.

You can read about how God knows you better
than anyone else in Psalm 139:1–6, 23–24.

DAY 3

GOD'S BOOK

God blessed them. . . . God saw all that he had made, and it was very good.

GENESIS 1:28, 31

It was a warm, sunny day, so Stacey decided to go for a walk. Not far from her house, a little boy stopped her and said, "My name is Genesis, and I'm six and a half years old."

"Genesis is a great name! It's a book in the Bible," Stacey replied.

"What's the Bible?" Genesis asked.

Stacey told him, "It's God's book about how He made the world and people and how He loves us."

Curious, he asked, "Why did He make the world and people and cars and houses? Is my picture in His book?"

We know there's no actual picture of us in the Bible, but we *are* all part of God's book. We read in the first book of the Bible, Genesis, that "God created mankind [all people] in his own image, in the image of God he created them" (1:27). God walked and talked with Adam and Eve in the garden and asked them not to eat from one special tree. They didn't listen (chapter 2)—and we still have trouble listening today.

Later in His book, we read about how Jesus came to teach us about Him and make a way for us to be forgiven. When we read the Bible, we learn that God wants us to know and love Him and even ask Him questions. He loves us more than we can imagine.

What is the best part of God's book?

Thank you for creating me, God.
And thanks for forgiving me.

You can read about how God created the
first people in Genesis 1:26–31.

DAY 4

"LOVE YOU-WHOLE WORLD"

Whoever lives in love lives in God, and God in them.

1 JOHN 4:16

When Jenna was three years old, she had an expression that melted her aunt's heart. If she really loved something— like chocolate chip cookies, jumping on the trampoline, or playing Frisbee—she'd exclaim, "I love it—whole world!" and then dramatically sweep out her arms.

What do you love like that? Your grandma? Your best friend? Your puppy? Pizza?

John, one of Jesus's disciples, wrote, "God is love." And he repeated it more than once because he wanted us to know it's true. God loves us very much. Much more than we could ever love anyone or anything. He loved us so much that Jesus died on the cross for our sins—the wrong and hurtful things we do.

God's love is like a flashlight or porch light that shines in the darkness. He sees our motives and knows if we're being selfish or out for revenge. But we don't need to be afraid. He still loves us.

When Jenna told her aunt, "I love you—whole world!" her aunt whispered back, "I love you—whole world!" And her aunt was reminded of how much God loves her. You can be sure of the same thing: God loves you—whole world!

What's your favorite thing about God's love?

Thank you for loving me, God,
even when I do what I know is wrong.

You can read about God's love in 1 John 4:7–12, 16–19.

DAY 5

DON'T FORGET ME!

He was taken up before their very eyes, and a cloud hid him from their sight.

ACTS 1:9

Anna and her four-year-old niece Kailyn had a fun Saturday afternoon together. They blew bubbles, colored in a princess coloring book, and ate peanut butter and jelly sandwiches. When Kailyn's mom picked her up to head home, the sweet girl called out the opened car window, "Don't forget me, Auntie Anna." Anna rushed to the window and said, "I could never forget you. I promise I'll see you soon."

After Jesus died on the cross, He rose again and spent forty more days with the disciples. Then He "was taken up [ascended] before their very eyes" into the sky (Acts 1:9). But before He left, Jesus promised to send His Spirit to live in them and help them (v. 8). He was going away to prepare a home for them and would come back and take them to be with Him (John 14:3). Yet they must

have wondered how long they would have to wait. Maybe they wanted to say, "Don't forget us, Jesus!"

If you believe in Jesus, He lives in you through the Holy Spirit. And one day He's coming back. We don't know when that will be, but it will happen. He won't forget us. Tell your friends about how much Jesus loves them so they can be with Him too.

If you could tell a friend about Jesus, what would you say?

Jesus, thank you for loving me and preparing a place just for me.

You can read about Jesus's last days with His disciples in Acts 1:3–11.

DAY 6

GIFTS FROM ABOVE

The virgin will conceive and give birth to a son, and they will call him Immanuel (which means "God with us").

MATTHEW 1:23

According to an old story, a man named Nicholas (born long ago in AD 270) heard about a father who was so poor he couldn't feed his three daughters or pay for their future marriages. Wanting to help the father, but hoping to keep it a secret, Nicholas threw a bag of gold through an open window. The gold landed in a shoe drying on the hearth. That man was known as Saint Nicholas, the inspiration for Santa Claus.

Did you know God gave us an even greater gift? Out of love and compassion, God sent to earth the greatest gift, His Son, through a miraculous birth. According to the gospel of Matthew, Jesus fulfilled the Old Testament prophecy that a virgin would give birth to a son called Immanuel, meaning "God with us" (1:23).

The gift of Jesus is far more amazing than any gift you could ever receive. Jesus left heaven to become a man, died and rose again. He is now in heaven. If we accept his gift of forgiveness, we will join him there someday.

What do you think is the most amazing thing about Jesus?

Jesus, thank you for coming to earth to save me from my sins.

You can read about the birth of Jesus in Matthew 1:18–25.

DAY 7

A CHEERFUL HEART

A cheerful heart is good medicine, but a broken spirit saps a person's strength.

PROVERBS 17:22 NLT

Lizzie's family has a "joke night" every week. Each of the four kids brings jokes to tell at dinner, and they have lots of fun and laughter around the table. The whole family loves it, and it helps Lizzie feel better when she's had a bad day at school or plans with a friend are canceled.

C. S. Lewis, the author of The Chronicles of Narnia, wrote about the benefits of laughter at dinnertime: "The sun looks down on nothing half so good as a household laughing together over a meal."

In Proverbs, a book in the Bible of wise sayings, we read about what it means to have a joyful attitude: "A cheerful heart is good medicine, but a broken spirit saps a person's strength" (17:22 NLT). This proverb gives us one way to stay healthy and strong, and it doesn't involve push-ups or getting a shot. When we have joy in our hearts, it can help us to be less upset when we argue with a friend. It can also help us to feel calm, even after a stressful test at school, and to feel loved by family and friends. The best reason to have joy? Jesus loves you!

The Bible encourages us to be cheerful. It does our body and heart good.

How do you think being cheerful helps you?

Dear God, I'm so glad you gave us laughter.

You can read about a cheerful heart and other wise sayings in Proverbs 17:19–22.

DAY 8

TWO ARE BETTER

Two are better than one, because they have a good return for their labor.

ECCLESIASTES 4:9

In the 1997 Ironman Triathlon in Hawaii, two women fought to stay on their feet as they hobbled toward the finish line. They ran on wobbly legs until Sian Welch bumped into Wendy Ingraham and they both dropped to the ground. Struggling to stand, they stumbled forward but fell again not far from the finish line. When Wendy began to crawl, the crowd applauded. They cheered even louder when Sian did the same.

Wendy crossed the finish line in fourth place and slumped into the arms of her supporters. Then she turned and reached out to help Sian. Sian lunged her body forward, stretching her arm toward Wendy's hand, and completed the race in fifth place.

Wendy's and Sian's dramatic finish of the 140-mile swimming, biking, and running race was exciting. They're also

a good example of the proverb, "Two are better than one" (Ecclesiastes 4:9). They helped each other to succeed.

It's okay to admit we need help from others—and from God. He already knows what we need. Sometimes we need help learning a new skill, making a tough decision, or knowing what to do when someone hurts our feelings. God hears our prayers. He's provided parents, teachers, friends, and others to help us succeed and to lift us up when we make mistakes. We're not alone.

Who can you go to when you need help?

Dear God, I need help with _____.

You can read about the advantages of having a friend or helper in Ecclesiastes 4:9–11.

DAY 9

FOR SUCH A TIME AS THIS

Who knows but that you have come to your royal position for such a time as this?

ESTHER 4:14

Tammie Jo Shults was piloting a plane for Southwest Airlines when, suddenly, one of the plane's two engines exploded. Pieces of the engine flew through a window, and Tammie Jo was forced to make a rapid descent from more than half a mile up in the sky. Thankfully, she safely landed the plane. She wasn't even supposed to be piloting that flight. She'd switched flights so she could attend her son's track meet. Tammie Jo had no idea she would be making an emergency landing that saved many people.

Esther was a young Jewish woman who lived during Old Testament times and became queen of Persia. She never dreamed she would be used by God to save others. When Esther learned her people's lives were in danger, she risked her own life to save theirs. She bravely did what she had to do. She asked the king to "spare my people" (Esther 7:3). God made Esther a queen "for such a time as this" (4:14) so her people would live.

One day God might use you to save others. We don't know His plans for us, but that's okay. If you're willing, God can use you to help others in big and small ways.

What do you like about Esther's story?

God, I want to help others. Like Esther, help me to be ready and willing.

You can read about Esther's story in Esther 4:10–17.

DAY 10

GOOD FOR YOU

Wisdom is like honey for you: If you find it,
there is a future hope.

PROVERBS 24:14

People around the world spend billions of dollars on chocolate each year. Imagine that! That's a lot of chocolate. But when you think about it, it's not all that surprising. Chocolate gives a boost of energy and tastes yummy—at least lots of people think so. Recently, scientists learned the sweet treat was also good for you.

Now you can tell your parents that chocolate contains flavonoids that help the body fight against aging and heart disease. But don't give up eating tangerines and apples!

King Solomon wrote about another "sweet." He told his son to eat honey "for it is good" (Proverbs 24:13) and compared its sweetness to wisdom. If we learn about and follow God's wisdom in the Bible, we discover it's not only good for the body but it also helps to prepare us for the good things we need to accomplish in life.

Wisdom helps us make smart choices and understand the world around us. Who doesn't want that? When we're wise, we make better decisions about who to hang out with and whether we should follow a friend's lead. We learn to ask: Is this a wise choice? We can feel good about feasting on God's wisdom in the Bible. It's a sweet treat we can enjoy without limit—in fact, God wants us to!

Why do you think it's good to learn about wisdom?

God, thank you for giving us the Bible.
I want to learn to be wise.

You can read about how wisdom is sweet
like honey in Proverbs 24:13–14.

DAY 11

TONGUE TAMERS

Do not let any unwholesome talk come out of your mouths, but only what is helpful for building others up.

EPHESIANS 4:29

In the book *West with the Night*, the author tells about Camciscan, a feisty stallion she hoped to tame. No matter what she tried, she could never fully tame the proud stallion. He was too stubborn and willful.

Ever feel that way about the things you say? Do you say mean things to your brother or sister or talk back to your mom or dad? The book of James compares the tongue to the bit in a horse's mouth or a ship's rudder, both used for steering (James 3:3–5). They're small but very important. Trouble comes if they're not handled with care.

How do we learn to watch what we say? The apostle Paul tells us to speak only the truth. And not to "let any unwholesome talk come out of your mouths, but only what is helpful for building others up" (Ephesians 4:29).

God wants us to speak the truth not to hurt others but to help them, and He wants us to think before we speak.

It took lots of hard work and patience to tame Camciscan. Taming the tongue isn't easy either. But you have the Bible's good advice and the Holy Spirit inside you. If you pray, God will help you. Don't give up!

When do you have the most trouble watching what you say?

Dear God, I don't want to say mean or nasty things. Please help me to stop and think before I speak.

You can read about the tongue in James 3:1–6 and Ephesians 4:25–29.

NEVER FORGOTTEN

See, I have engraved you on the palms of my hands.

ISAIAH 49:16

Lisa's kids bugged their mom to prove she had years of piano lessons. She sat down and started playing the C major scale. After nearly twenty years, she was surprised she remembered! Feeling brave, she played seven different scales by heart, one right after the other. Years of practicing had imprinted the notes and technique so deeply in her fingers' "memory" that they instantly knew what to do.

It's hard to forget some things, like riding a bike or that song that's stuck in your head. But God's love for us is far more deeply imprinted or stuck than any memory. God can't forget us! The Israelites needed to hear that when they were carried away to Babylon and thought God had forgotten them. The message God gave them was clear: "I will not forget you!" (Isaiah 49:15). God's promise to care for His people was more certain than a parent's love for a daughter.

To assure them of His never-ending love, God told them: "See, I have engraved you on the palms of my hands" (v. 16). God loves and knows His children. He can't forget their names and faces. If you believe in God, you're His child too.

When you feel overlooked or forgotten, know that you're stamped on God's hands—always remembered, cared for, and loved by Him.

How does it feel to know God will never forget you?

Dear God, thank you for loving me forever!

You can read about God's never-ending love for you in Isaiah 49:8–16.

DAY 13

WORDS THAT WOUND

The words of the reckless pierce like swords,
but the tongue of the wise brings healing.

PROVERBS 12:18

As Alicia walked to school, the neighbor boy ran up to her and taunted, "Skinny bones, skinny bones!" Alicia was shy and self-conscious. Even if she could have chanted, "Sticks and stones may break my bones, but words will never hurt me," it wouldn't have helped. She knew it wasn't true. Bullying and mean words hurt.

Adults can hurt each other with words too. Hannah knew the sting of thoughtless words. Her husband, Elkanah, loved her, but she had no children. His second wife, Peninnah, had many. In a culture where a woman was valuable if she had children (and when a husband could have more than one wife!), Peninnah made Hannah's pain worse by continually mocking her for being childless. She kept it up until Hannah wept and couldn't eat. Hannah turned to God in prayer, and He heard.

Have you ever been bullied? Has someone said something mean that really hurt your feelings? Instead of lashing out and saying nasty things back, God wants you to run to Him for comfort. He can help you to face mean words because He thinks you are precious. You are loved.

What do you do when someone says mean things to you?

Dear God, help me come to you when I'm hurt by someone's words. Help me to know what to say and do.

You can read about Hannah's story in 1 Samuel 1:1–18.

DAY 14

GOD IS WITH YOU

The Lord opened the servant's eyes, and he . . . [saw]
chariots of fire all around Elisha.

2 KINGS 6:17

In C. S. Lewis's book *The Lion, the Witch and the Wardrobe*, the people of Narnia were thrilled when the mighty lion Aslan reappeared after a long absence. Their joy turned to sadness, however, when Aslan appeared to be defeated by the evil White Witch. He wasn't! He let out an earsplitting roar that caused the witch to flee in terror. Aslan was much greater than the wicked witch.

Like Aslan's followers, Elisha's servant despaired when he got up one morning to see they were surrounded by an enemy army. "Oh no, my lord! What shall we do?" he exclaimed (2 Kings 6:15). Elisha calmly responded, "Don't be afraid. . . . Those who are with us are more than those who are with them" (v. 16). Then he prayed, "Open his eyes, LORD, so that he may see" (v. 17). So, "the LORD opened the servant's eyes, and he looked and

saw the hills full of horses and chariots of fire all around Elisha" (v. 17).

If you're facing a difficult situation, don't be afraid. God is much greater and more powerful than any enemy or circumstance. And you're never alone. He is with you.

What fear are you facing right now?

Thank you, God, for being greater than any person or any problem. Help me to trust you.

You can read about Elisha, his servant, and God's power in 2 Kings 6:8–17.

SEEING CLEARLY

Then his eyes were opened, his sight was restored, and he saw everything clearly.

MARK 8:25

When Julie got glasses, her dad said, "It must be awesome to look at a tree and see the individual leaves instead of just a blur of green!" Julie wasn't excited about needing to wear glasses, but it was great to finally see clearly!

When we read the Bible, certain books and stories can seem like looking at trees without glasses. They appear to be just simple stories or, worse, boring details. But looking closer can open our eyes to what the words are saying.

In Mark 8, we read about how Jesus healed a blind man. Jesus healed others, but this story is different. He didn't simply say a word or touch the man to heal him. He did two things. First, Jesus put spit on the man's eyes and asked, "Do you see anything?" (v. 23). The man replied, "I see people; they look like trees walking around" (v. 24).

Then Jesus touched him again, and the man "saw everything clearly" (v. 25).

When we become Christians, we don't suddenly understand everything about God or the Bible. We need to keep reading and look closer. Praying for understanding and asking questions help us get a clearer picture of how awesome God really is.

What is one thing about God or the Bible that you wish you understood better?

Dear God, please help me to know you better and understand you more.

You can read about how God healed a blind man in Mark 8:22–26.

DAY  **16**

YOU HAVE TO RELAX!

*Return to your rest, my soul, for the Lᴏʀᴅ
has been good to you.*

PSALM 116:7

Imagine going to the doctor's office to get stitches for a cut on your arm. The doctor stitching you up says, "Try to relax," not having numbed the area around your cut, and while waving the surgical needle in front of you! Would you be able to relax? Probably not.

If we're scared, someone telling us to relax doesn't help much. When our stomach is tied up in knots, our first instinct is to fight back, not relax. That usually only makes us more anxious. But when we give our fear and worry to God (Psalm 116:4), something surprising happens. The knot inside us begins to relax (v. 7), and a peace we can't understand rushes through us. That peace comes from God. He's given us the Holy Spirit to comfort us. We can give our fears to Him because He cares for us.

Are you worried or scared about something? A big science project, a new school, a bully? Pray about it. And don't forget that God has placed adults in your life who also care about you and can help.

When you're panicked, how does it help to know God cares for you?

Dear God, I'm worried about _____.
Please help me not to be anxious.

You can read about how God cares for you and hears your prayers in Psalm 116:1–9.

DAY 17

IN GOD'S IMAGE

God created mankind in his own image, in the image of God he created them; male and female he created them.

GENESIS 1:27

When her beautiful brown skin started losing its color, the young woman felt as if she were losing her "self." She covered up her "spots," as she called them, with heavy makeup. She has vitiligo, a condition that causes a loss of skin pigment, melanin, which gives skin its color. This results in patches of lighter skin.

She asked God to help her accept herself, and she stopped wearing heavy makeup. Soon she gained attention for her self-confidence. Eventually she became the first spokesmodel with vitiligo for a makeup company. "It's such a blessing," she told a TV news host, adding that she finds encouragement through her faith, family, and friends.

When God created people, He made us special: "God created mankind in his own image, in the image of God he created them; male and female he created them" (Genesis

1:27). No matter what we look like on the outside, as God's created persons, we look kind of like Him. And as believers in Jesus, He helps us to shine His light to other people.

Do you struggle to love yourself? Remember, you are God's child, and He loves you. You can look in the mirror and smile for God.

How does it help to know you are made in God's image?

Dear God, help me to love myself as I am and to remember that you think I'm special.

You can read about the creation of the first people in Genesis 1:26–31.

DAY 18

BEAR HUG

We love because he first loved us.

1 JOHN 4:19

Elisa gave her grandson a giant stuffed animal named "Bear." Baby D responded with wonder and amazement. Then curiosity nudged him into daring exploration. He poked his pudgy finger at Bear's nose. When Bear tumbled forward into his arms, Baby D responded with joy!

Baby D laid his toddler head down on Bear's fluffy chest and hugged him tightly. A smile spread across his cheeks as he burrowed deeply into Bear's cushiony softness. The little boy had no idea that Bear could not truly love him. He felt love from Bear and returned it with all his heart.

In a letter to early Christians, the apostle John wrote that God himself is love. "We know and rely on the love God has for us," he wrote. "God is love" (1 John 4:16). God loves. Not like a stuffed animal that can't love us back but with the outstretched arms of someone who loved us so much He died for our sins so we could be with Him forever.

Through Jesus, God showed His extravagant love for us. John says, "We love because he first loved us" (v. 19). When we believe we're loved, we love back. God's real love makes it possible for us to love God and others with all our heart.

What do you love best about God?

Dear God, thank you for loving me! Help me to love you more.

You can read about God's love for you in 1 John 4:13–19.

DAY 19

EVERYONE NEEDS COMPASSION

When he saw the crowds, he had compassion on them,
because they were harassed and helpless, like sheep
without a shepherd.

MATTHEW 9:36

When Jeff was a new believer in Jesus and just out of college, he worked for a big company. As a salesman, he traveled a lot. As he did, he heard many heartbreaking stories. He realized that what people needed most wasn't the product he was selling, but compassion. They needed God. This led Jeff to attend seminary to learn more about God and to become a pastor.

In Matthew 9:27–33 we see Christ's compassion in the healing of two blind men and one demon-possessed man. During His ministry on earth, Jesus went through the towns and villages preaching the gospel and healing. Why? "When he saw the crowds, he had compassion on them, because they were harassed and helpless, like sheep without a shepherd" (v. 36).

The world today is full of troubled and hurting people who need Jesus. Like a shepherd who guides and protects his sheep, Jesus cares for everyone who comes to Him—and that means you too. When you pray about your troubles, He hears and surrounds you with His love and tenderness. He cares. If you've felt God's loving compassion, you'll want to be loving and kind to others.

How can you show compassion to
a friend or family member?

*Dear God, I want to be more like you.
Help me to be kind to others.*

You can read about Jesus's compassion
in Matthew 9:27–38.

HOW TO REFLECT CHRIST

God has chosen to make known . . . the glorious riches of this mystery, which is Christ in you, the hope of glory.

COLOSSIANS 1:27

Thérèse was a happy little girl—until her mother died when she was just four years old. She became shy and was easily upset. Years later, on Christmas Eve, all of that changed. After celebrating the birth of Jesus with the people of her church, she felt God taking away her fear and giving her joy. She owed the change to God living in her.

What does it mean for Christ to live in you? It's a mystery, Paul told the Colossian church (Colossians 1:26), but one that God made known to His people when Jesus came to earth as a man. Because Christ now lived in the Colossian people in the form of the Holy Spirit, they experienced the joy of new life. Sin and pain and fear no longer controlled them.

If you've asked Jesus to be your Savior, Jesus lives in you. Through His Spirit, He can remove your fear and worry, as He did for Thérèse. And because He lives in you, He helps you to be more like Him.

What does it mean that Jesus is living inside you?

Dear God, help me to grow more like you every day.

You can read about the mystery of Christ in us in Colossians 1:25–27.

DAY 21

EAT AND REPEAT

We have lost our appetite; we never see anything but this manna!

NUMBERS 11:6

"I'm sick of the same food all the time!" Kerry complained. Her mom seemed to make the same boring meals every week. Kerry's mom and dad weren't happy with her. For the next three days, twelve-year-old Kerry was in charge of dinner. On the first night, Kerry made spaghetti. But she made way too much. So she served it again the next night. On the third night, as she thought about what to make, she realized she only knew how to make spaghetti. She went to her mom and apologized. "Mom, I'm sorry. You're a good cook, and I'm tired of spaghetti."

Just imagine eating the same meal as the Israelites did—for forty years. Each morning they gathered the sweet "super food" (manna) God supplied and cooked it. They got creative by baking it and boiling it (Exodus 16:23).

But they missed the good food they'd enjoyed in Egypt, even though they'd been enslaved there!

Do you sometimes dislike the sameness of your life? The same boring food or school? Exodus 16 tells how God, by giving the Israelites just what they needed for each day, helped them to trust and depend on His care. God promises to give you everything you need. He loves you and knows what's best. And don't worry, your life won't always be the same.

Why do you think God wants you to
be happy with what you have?

Dear God, help me to be content.

You can read about manna in Exodus 16:14–18.

DAY 22

TRUE FRIENDS

A friend loves at all times.

PROVERBS 17:17

In middle school, Diana had a "sometimes friend" named Clarissa. They hung out at the small church they attended and sometimes outside of school. But in school, if Clarissa met Diana, Clarissa might say hello—but only if no one else was around. She was part of the popular crowd; Diana wasn't. So Diana didn't try to talk to her at school. She knew the limits of their friendship.

Have you ever had a one-sided friendship? It hurts to know you like the other person more than they like you. Thankfully, there's another kind of friendship—one that has no limits. It's the kind of friendship we have with others who love us no matter what. David and Jonathan were friends like that.

Jonathan was "one in spirit" with David and loved him "as himself" (1 Samuel 18:1). Even though Jonathan should have become king after his father Saul's death, God had chosen David to be the next king. Jonathan chose to be loyal to David, and even helped him to escape Saul's plots to kill him.

Despite everything, Jonathan and David remained friends. They showed the truth of Proverbs 17:17: "A friend loves at all times." Through faithful friendships like theirs, we get a better understanding of God's never-ending love for us.

Why is it good to know God loves you even more than a best friend or parent?

Dear God, help me to find a true friend and to know your love never ends.

You can read about David and Jonathan's friendship in 1 Samuel 18:1–4; 19:1–6.

DAY 23

DIRTY FEET

I have set you an example that you should do as I have done for you.

JOHN 13:15

Laura and her mom were headed home after an afternoon of school shopping and then dinner at Laura's favorite restaurant. But the car sputtered as her mom turned the key. A man in the parking lot noticed, and asked if he could help. He jump-started her car, and soon Laura and her mom were headed home. The man took the time to care for a stranger in need by serving in the way Jesus asks us to serve.

In John 13:5 Jesus "poured water into a basin and began to wash his disciples' feet." Washing feet filthy from walking the dirt roads of Jerusalem in sandals was a servant's job. When Peter questioned Jesus's actions, Jesus explained that this is how He wants us to treat each another: "I have set you an example that you should do as I have

done for you" (v. 15). His action demonstrates how we're to serve others.

Jesus doesn't expect us to wash others' feet. Serving others could mean baking brownies for a neighbor or raking their leaves. It could be helping your mom with your younger sister or brother, even if you'd rather be with your friends. Jesus's actions show how much He cares for us, and He asks us to do kind things for others.

What could you do today to help someone?

Jesus, I want to be more like you. Help me to be kind.

You can read about how Jesus served
His disciples in John 13:4–17.

BLUE LINES

I instruct you in the way of wisdom and lead you along straight paths.

PROVERBS 4:11

Do you like to ski? Did you know downhill skiing racecourses are often marked by lines of blue paint sprayed across the white, snowy surface? The paint serves as a guide for the racers to find the fastest way to the bottom of the hill. The contrast of the paint against the snow also helps racers with depth perception, which is critical to their safety when traveling at high rates of speed.

In the Old Testament, King Solomon begs his sons to seek wisdom in hopes of keeping them safe on the racecourse of life. Like the blue lines, wisdom, he says, will "lead [them] along straight paths" and keep them from stumbling (Proverbs 4:11–12). His deepest hope as a father is for his sons to enjoy a good life, free from the damaging effects of ignoring the wisdom of God.

God, our loving Father, offers us "blue-line" guidance. When we choose to follow God and what He teaches us in the Bible, He helps us to make wise choices each day. His wisdom guides us to choose the right friends and to obey our parents and so much more.

What wise decision might you choose today?

Dear God, please help me to make the right choices each day.

You can read about wisdom in Proverbs 4:10–15.

DAY **25**

GOD PROVIDES

See how the flowers of the field grow. . . .
Will [God] not much more clothe you?

MATTHEW 6:28, 30

Li and her friends trekked deep into the forest and farther away from their village in China. After an hour or so, Li heard the deafening roar of water. Soon they reached a clearing and spied a beautiful waterfall cascading over gray rocks. Li's hiking buddies, who lived in the village they'd left an hour earlier, told her it was time for a picnic. Li was hungry, but they hadn't brought any food.

As Li enjoyed the view, her friends disappeared into the forest and returned with an assortment of fruits and vegetables and even some fish. One strange-looking plant had small purple flowers, but it tasted delicious!

Li was reminded of how God provides for all His creatures. He created "all sorts of seed-bearing plants, and trees with seed-bearing fruit" (Genesis 1:12 NLT). God made and gave us an amazing variety of plants and trees with edible and yummy seeds, fruits, and vegetables.

Do you sometimes find it hard to believe God cares about you and your needs? In the New Testament, Jesus tells you not to worry about food or clothes. God knows exactly what you need. You can trust Him to provide.

What in nature reminds you of God's care for you?

Dear God, thank you for all the variety of fruit and vegetables you created just for us.

You can read about the creation of plants in Genesis 1:11–13, 29–30.

DAY 26

THE FAVORITE

As I have loved you, so you must love one another.

JOHN 13:34

Gerrits and his family live hundreds of miles away from the rest of his grown siblings and their families. Despite the distance, Gerrits has always been a loved family member because of his humor and kind heart. His siblings joke about his favored status in their mother's eyes. Several years ago, they even gave him a T-shirt that said, "I'm Mom's Favorite." They're just being silly, but true favoritism is no joking matter.

In Genesis 37, we read about Jacob, who gave his son Joseph a beautiful coat. Nice, right? The thing is, Jacob had eleven other sons. His gift shouted: "Joseph is my favorite son!" Displaying favoritism can be crippling in a family. Jacob's action set the stage for Joseph's brothers to despise their younger brother, even plotting his murder.

When it comes to our friends and family members, it can be hard to treat everyone the same. It's natural to

like some people more than others. But God wants us to treat everyone fairly and to love the people in our life as our heavenly Father loves us. How can you do that today?

What's one way you can love others
without showing favoritism?

*Dear God, help me to treat my family
members and friends with fairness.*

You can read about the danger of
favoritism in Genesis 37:2–4, 17–24.

DAY 27

WATCHED BY GOD

The Lord watches over you.

PSALM 121:5

Patricia's grandson headed for the car, then turned back and asked, "Grandma, why do you stand on the porch and watch until we leave?" Seeing his concern, she told him, "Well, it's a courtesy. If you're my guest, watching until you leave shows I care."

The little boy thought about it but still looked perplexed. So Patricia told him the simple truth. "I watch," she said, "because I love you. When I see your car drive away, I know you're safely heading home." He smiled and gave her a big hug.

Our heavenly Father always watches over us, His precious children. The Bible says, "The Lord watches over you—the Lord is your shade at your right hand" (Psalm 121:5). That truth helped the people of Israel feel safe as they climbed dangerous roads to Jerusalem to worship. The Lord was watching over their lives—and He watches over yours.

Isn't that comforting to know? God is with you now, and He will be with you as you grow. He'll help you to make wise decisions each step of the way. He loves you now and forever.

Why is it good to know God watches over you?

Dear God, thank you for loving and watching over me.

You can read about how God watches
over you in Psalm 121:5–8.

THE SECRET

*I have learned the secret of being content
in any and every situation.*

PHILIPPIANS 4:12

When Monica comes home from school, her cat Heathcliff rushes over to inspect her backpack. When she's snacking, he stands up on his back paws begging her to share. But when she gives Heathcliff whatever has caught his fancy, he quickly loses interest and walks away with an air of bored resentment.

In a way, Heathcliff is a picture of our own hunger for more, our discontent with what we have. It's like the little kid who's happily playing with a toy until he sees his brother playing with another toy and wants what he has.

According to the apostle Paul, contentment isn't natural. It's got to be learned. On our own, we want whatever we think will satisfy us—a TV in our bedroom, the coolest shoes. The minute we realize what we wanted didn't satisfy, we move on to the next thing.

Paul experienced lots of hard things—hunger, shipwreck, beatings, and more—but he'd learned to be content. He knew "the secret" of true contentment (Philippians 4:12). He trusted God. God is the one who takes away our worries and fears and gives us peace and strength. He satisfies our longings for more.

When do you feel discontent?

Dear God, help me to be satisfied with what I have.

You can read about what it means to be content in Philippians 4:6–13.

KINDNESS

I want to show God's kindness to them.

2 SAMUEL 9:3 NLT

When the young mom got on the plane with her kids, she wondered how she'd get through the trip. It wasn't long before her three-year-old daughter began kicking and crying. Then her hungry four-month-old son began to wail. Thankfully, the traveler seated next to her offered to hold the baby while Jessica got her daughter buckled in. Then he colored with the toddler while Jessica fed her infant.

Jessica recalled, "I [was] blown away by God's hand in this. [We] could have been placed next to anyone, but we were seated next to one of the nicest men I have ever met."

In 2 Samuel 9, we read about another example of kindness. After King Saul and his son Jonathan were killed in battle, people expected King David to get rid of any competitors to his claim for the throne. Instead, David asked if Saul had any living relatives he could show God's kindness to.

Jonathan had one son, Mephibosheth, still alive. David gave him the land that had been his grandfather's and invited him to eat at his table from then on—as if he were his own son.

Has someone shown kindness to you or your family? How did it feel? Imagine all the ways you can show kindness to others.

When has someone been really kind to you?

Dear God, thank you for examples of kindness we learn about in the Bible.

You can read about Mephibosheth in 2 Samuel 9:3–11.

DAY 30

REUNION

Look! God's dwelling place is now among the people.

REVELATION 21:3

The little boy excitedly ripped open a big box from his daddy. He was in the military and living overseas. The little guy hadn't seen his daddy in months, so the present was very special. Inside that box was another gift-wrapped box, and inside that box was another that held a piece of paper saying, "Surprise!" Confused, the boy looked up—just as his dad entered the room. Tearfully the son leapt into his father's arms, exclaiming, "Daddy, I missed you!" and "I love you!"

That tearful yet joyful reunion is like the awesome moment in the future when we see Jesus in heaven. There, "[God] will wipe every tear from [our] eyes" (Revelation 21:4). We'll have no more pain or sorrow because we'll be with our heavenly Father.

If you're a follower of Jesus, you already have love and joy from God right now. But one day your joy will be over the top when Jesus welcomes you into His open arms! It will be better than getting that new video game you couldn't wait to have or taking that exciting vacation with your family. Just imagine, no more tears or pain. And you'll get to talk to Jesus face-to-face every day!

What do you think will be the best part about being with Jesus?

Jesus, right now I like living on this earth. But I'm happy that one day I'll be with you.

You can read about your new home with Jesus in Revelation 21:1–7.

DAY 31

WEAK KNEES

Strengthen the feeble hands, steady the knees that give way.

ISAIAH 35:3

When Linda was little, she thought the song she heard at church, "He Looked Beyond My Fault and Saw My Need," was "He Looked Beyond My Fault and Saw My Knees." She wondered why God would look at knees. Was it because they were weak? She knew weak-kneed meant "afraid."

Later, Linda learned that the songwriter, Dottie Rambo, wrote it for her brother Eddie. He believed he was unlovable because of the bad things he'd done. Dottie sang to him about God's unconditional, never-ending love. The song assured Eddie that God saw his weakness but loved him anyway.

God shows unconditional love throughout the Bible. He sent lots of prophets like Isaiah with messages for His people to come back to Him. In Isaiah 35, the prophet told them

God would "strengthen the feeble hands, steady the knees that give way" (v. 3). He encouraged them not to be afraid but to be strong. Through the encouragement they received, God's people could then encourage others.

Do you ever worry that God doesn't love you? When you read the Bible, the message is clear—He does! Talk to Him in prayer and be encouraged.

What's the best thing about knowing God loves you?

Dear God, help me to know you forgive and love me—and won't ever stop loving me.

You can read about God's love in Isaiah 35:1–4.

DAY **32**

THE CREATOR CARES

The Son is the radiance of God's glory . . . sustaining all things by his powerful word.

HEBREWS 1:3

Today most people rely on their phone to tell the time, but before cell phones people depended on watches. Some still do. And Swiss watches are among the best. These specialty watches are made of many tiny pieces, but the essential part is the mainspring. The mainspring moves all the gears to allow the watch to keep time. Without it, even the best-designed watch won't work.

In the book of Hebrews, the unknown writer praises Jesus for creating the heavens and the earth. Like the intricacy of a specialty watch, every detail of our universe was created by Jesus. From the vastness of the solar system to the uniqueness of our fingerprints, all things were made by Him.

Jesus, like a clock's mainspring, is also responsible for making creation function and flourish. He "[sustains]

all things by his powerful word" (Hebrews 1:3), which means He keeps everything He created working together.

When you're out in nature, you get a small glimpse of God's beautiful creation. When you see a sparkling lake or pretty flower, remember that Jesus, the creator and sustainer of the universe, cares and provides for you.

What do you think is the best part of God's creation?

Jesus, thank you for creating the universe and everything in it. And thank you for caring for me.

You can read about Jesus's role in creation in Hebrews 1:1–4.

DAY 33

THE LORD WILL PROVIDE

So Abraham called that place The Lord Will Provide.

GENESIS 22:14

Julie was worried. In a few weeks she would be starting middle school. She'd known everyone in her old school, but now she'd be in classes with kids she might not know. Plus, she'd have different teachers for every class—and a locker. What if she forgot her locker combination or got lost? Then Julie learned she'd have an orientation day and could see where her locker and each of her classes were. She would even get to meet her new teachers, and she felt relieved. She remembered that God would be with her.

Abraham went through a far more difficult situation. He was asked to take his son and sacrifice him on a mountain. Abraham obeyed God and took Isaac there. The three-day journey gave Abraham plenty of time to change his mind, but he didn't. When Isaac questioned his father, Abraham replied, "God himself will provide the lamb for the burnt offering" (Genesis 22:8).

Abraham's anxiety probably grew with each knot he tied as he bound Isaac. What a relief it must have been when the angel stopped him! God provided a ram, caught in the tangled weeds, as a sacrifice. God tested Abraham's faith, and he proved faithful. And at the right time, to the very second, God provided.

If you're worried, pray about whatever's bothering you. God will provide.

What are you worried about right now?

God, I'm worried about _____. Please help.

You can read about Abraham and Isaac in Genesis 22:2–14.

THE ONLY KING

They bowed down and worshiped him.

MATTHEW 2:11

As five-year-old Eldon listened to the pastor talk about Jesus, he gasped when the pastor thanked Him in prayer for dying for our sins. "Oh, no! He died?" the boy said in surprise.

From the start of Christ's life on earth, there were some people who wanted Him dead. Wise men came to Jerusalem during the reign of King Herod and asked, "Where is the one who has been born king of the Jews? We saw his star when it rose and have come to worship him" (Matthew 2:2).

When the king heard it, he was afraid Jesus would one day rule in his place. So he sent soldiers to kill all the boys two years old and younger around Bethlehem. But God protected His Son and sent an angel to warn His parents. They fled, and He was saved.

When Jesus completed His ministry, He was crucified for the sins of the world. Yet three days later He rose in victory from the grave. After ascending to heaven, He sat down on the throne as King of kings and Lord of lords. The King died for our sins. If you haven't already, you can ask Him to rule in your heart.

Why are you thankful for Jesus?

Jesus, thank you for coming to earth and for living and dying for me.

You can read about Herod and the wise men in Matthew 2:1–12.

DAY 35

LED BY HIS WORD

Direct my footsteps according to your word;
let no sin rule over me.

PSALM 119:133

Paul Arnold's first job on radio was making "walking sounds" in radio dramas. While actors read from scripts during a walking scene, Paul made the sounds of walking with his feet—matching his pace to the actor's voice and spoken lines. The key challenge, he explained, was to follow the actor's lead, "so the two of us were working together."

Did you know God wants you to work together with Him? To do this, you get to know God through reading the Bible and prayer, and then, with His help, you do the things that please Him. As Psalm 119:1 says, "Blessed are those whose ways are blameless, who walk according to the law of the LORD." When we let God lead the way and follow His instructions, He helps us to do the right things, find good friends, and be joyful.

Before you do or say something you're unsure about or may regret, read what the Bible says about it. Is it something Jesus might do? If unsure, ask your parents. When you follow His example, He helps you to walk so closely with Him that people see Jesus in you!

Why do you think it's important to read the Bible?

Dear God, help me to do good things that please you.

You can read about how God wants you
to live in Psalm 119:1, 133–136.

DAY **36**

RELENTLESS LOVE

*Let us not love with words or speech
but with actions and in truth.*

1 JOHN 3:18

Do you remember the first time you saw snow? Heidi and Jeff came home from working overseas in a hot climate and lived for several months near family in the state of Michigan—just in time for winter. It would be the first time many of their ten kids experienced snow; and winter weather in Michigan requires a lot of warm clothes, including coats, mittens, and boots. For a large family, it would be expensive to outfit them for the bitterly cold months ahead.

But God provided. First, a neighbor brought over boots, snow pants, hats, and gloves. Then, a friend urged others at her church to collect a variety of warm clothes in all twelve sizes for each member of the family. By the time the snow arrived, the family had exactly what they needed.

Did you know you can serve God by helping others? Serving helps you to be more like Jesus as you begin to love and see people as He does. As you serve, you're also encouraged. And your faith in God grows. Serving can mean helping a neighbor rake leaves, baking cookies for a friend, or offering to help your mom with a chore. You don't need money to serve and show someone God's love.

How could you serve someone today?

Dear God, help me to want to do things for other people.

You can read about serving in 1 John 3:16–18.

EYES TO SEE

Open my eyes that I may see wonderful things in your law.

PSALM 119:18

In a video on social media, Tommy, a visually impaired toddler, sits on his father's lap in a doctor's office. When the eye doctor rests a tiny pair of glasses on his nose, Tommy's eyes fly open. He points to the light in the ceiling and then at a toy on the floor. Finally, he turns to face his daddy. When their eyes meet, Tommy's little mouth drops open, and he sucks in a breath. "Dada!" he exclaims.

You're probably not legally blind like Tommy, but you may have trouble seeing how God works in you and in the world. Perhaps you think the Bible is just another boring book, or you don't see how loving and good God is.

If you pray for God to open your eyes, He can do amazing things. He can help you understand what you're reading in the Bible, and He can help you want to do good things.

God can also give you the desire to read Scripture, and He can help you see Him at work on every page.

Tommy needed a doctor's help to see with his physical eyes. We need God's help, every day, to see the wonders He has provided in Scripture. And don't forget, God gave us pastors and others to help us too.

What do you need help with when you read the Bible?

Dear God, help me to want to read the Bible and to get to know you better.

You can read about how special God's words are in Psalm 119:11–19.

DAY 38

WATCH ME!

From the lips of children and infants you, Lord,
have called forth your praise.

MATTHEW 21:16

"Watch my fairy princess dance, Sophia!" three-year-old Moriah called out to her big sister as she raced around the yard of the cabin, a huge grin on her face. Her "dancing" made Sophia smile. Just watching Moriah's joy at being on vacation made her big sister happy too!

The first Palm Sunday long ago was a day of highs and lows. When Jesus rode into Jerusalem on a donkey, the crowds called out, "Hosanna!" and "Blessed is he who comes in the name of the Lord!" Yet many people in the crowd were expecting a leader to free them from a cruel government, not a Savior who would die for their sins.

Later that day, despite the anger of some leaders, children in the temple were joyfully shouting, "Hosanna to the Son of David" (Matthew 21:15), perhaps leaping and waving

palm branches as they ran around the courtyard. They couldn't help but worship Jesus!

God loves to hear your praise! You can shout and sing and even dance for Him. Can you picture God smiling?

Why do you think God likes to hear your praise?

Jesus, thank you for coming to save me from my sins. I love you!

You can read about Palm Sunday in Matthew 21:12–17.

DAY 39

OUT OF THE MOUTHS OF BABES

Out of the mouth of babies and infants, you have established strength because of your foes.

PSALM 8:2 ESV

After watching ten-year-old Viola use a tree branch as a microphone to pretend to be a preacher, Michele decided to give Viola the opportunity to "preach" during a village outreach. Viola accepted. Michele, a missionary in South Sudan, wrote, "The crowd was enraptured" as the girl shared about Jesus. "Half the crowd came forward to receive Jesus."

The crowd didn't expect to hear a young girl preach. But good things happened because she did. In Psalm 8, the psalmist David wrote, "Out of the mouth of babies and infants, you have established strength because of your foes" (v. 2 ESV). Jesus later quoted this verse after the church leaders—chief priests and scribes—criticized the children for praising Jesus in the temple at Jerusalem (Matthew 21:16). The leaders considered these children annoying. By quoting this verse, Jesus showed that God took these children seriously. They did what the leaders were unwilling to do: give praise to Jesus, who came to bring salvation to all who believe in Him.

As Viola and the children in the temple showed, God can use kids like you to tell others about Him. If you're willing, God will work in and through you.

What could you tell a friend about Jesus?

God, help me to tell others about you.

You can read about the children in the temple in Matthew 21:14–16.

DAY  **40**

WHO KNOWS?

When times are good, be happy; but when times are bad, consider this: God has made the one as well as the other.

ECCLESIASTES 7:14

According to Chinese legend, when Sai Weng lost track of one of his prized horses, his neighbor expressed his sorrow. But Sai Weng wasn't worried. He said, "Who knows if it may be a good thing for me?" Surprisingly, the lost horse returned home with another horse. As the neighbor congratulated him, Sai Weng said, "Who knows if it may be a bad thing for me?"

As it turned out, his son broke his leg when he rode the new horse. This seemed like a bad thing, until the army arrived at the village to recruit soldiers. Because of the son's injury, he wasn't recruited, which may have saved his life. This story illustrates the Chinese proverb: a difficulty can be a blessing in disguise and vice versa.

This ancient wisdom is like the words of Ecclesiastes 6:12: "Who knows what is good for a person in life?" Only

God knows what the future holds. As God's children, we can trust He is with us in good and bad times. God has "made the one as well as the other" (7:14). He's with us in all the events of our lives. He can bring good even out of the bad things that happen.

Why is it good to know God is always with you?

Dear God, help me to know you are with me even in bad times and that things will get better.

You can read more words of wisdom in Ecclesiastes 6:12; 7:13–14.

DAY 41

WHEN SHARKS WON'T BITE

One who is full loathes honey from the comb.

PROVERBS 27:7

Jennifer felt a little nervous. But her friends were thrilled. They were visiting an aquarium where people could pet small sharks kept in a special tank. When Jennifer asked if the sharks ever snapped at fingers, she was told the sharks had recently been fed and then given extra food. They wouldn't bite because they weren't hungry.

What Jennifer learned makes sense. "One who is full loathes honey from the comb, but to the hungry even what is bitter tastes sweet" (Proverbs 27:7). Hunger—a feeling of inner emptiness—can lead us to make bad decisions. God wants more for us than a life lived at the mercy of our stomachs or things we want. He wants us to be filled with Jesus's love so that everything we do comes out of the peace and strength He provides. Knowing we're loved gives us confidence. It helps us to choose friends wisely and to do the right things.

Get to know Jesus. You can find satisfaction in a friendship with Him. He provides all you really need.

Why do you think it's important to know Jesus?

Jesus, help me to get to know you better through reading the Bible.

You can read some sayings for wise living in Proverbs 27:1–10.

THE UNSEEN

Elisha prayed, "Open his eyes, LORD, so that he may see."
2 KINGS 6:17

Stephen Cass was curious about the invisible things that were part of his daily life. As he walked toward his office in New York City, he thought: "If I could see radio waves, the top of the Empire State Building [with all its radio and TV antennas] would be lit like a kaleidoscopic flare, illuminating the entire city." He realized he was surrounded by an invisible electromagnetic field of radio and TV signals, Wi-Fi, and more.

Elisha's servant learned about another kind of unseen reality—the invisible spiritual world. They were surrounded by an enemy army. Soldiers on warhorses were everywhere! The servant was afraid, but Elisha wasn't worried because he saw the powerful army of angels that surrounded their enemy. He told his servant, "Those who are with us are more than those who are with them" (2 Kings 6:16). Then he asked God to open his servant's eyes so he too could see. God was in control.

Do you sometimes feel helpless or afraid? Talk to your parents and pray about it. God is in control and fights for you. He "will command his angels concerning you to guard you in all your ways" (Psalm 91:11).

What's the best thing about this Bible story?

Dear God, help me to know you are on my side.

You can read about Elisha in 2 Kings 6:8–17.

DAY 43

A LEGACY OF FAITH

I am reminded of your sincere faith, which first lived in your grandmother Lois and in your mother Eunice.

2 TIMOTHY 1:5

Billy Graham's parents loved Jesus, and his grandparents did too. His parents prayed and read Scripture and attended church together with their kids. The solid foundation Billy's parents laid for him helped to bring Billy to faith at age sixteen and later to become an evangelist. He went all over the world telling people about Jesus.

The apostle Paul's young disciple Timothy also benefited from a strong spiritual foundation. Paul wrote, "Your sincere faith . . . first lived in your grandmother Lois and in your mother Eunice" (2 Timothy 1:5). This legacy helped prepare and steer Timothy's heart toward faith in Christ. And so, Paul urged Timothy to carry on this faith tradition, to "fan into flame the gift of God" within him through the Holy Spirit, who gives us power (vv. 6–7).

Because of the Spirit living inside him, Timothy could fearlessly live for Jesus.

Do your parents or grandparents believe in Jesus? Do you? If so, be thankful they helped lead you to Jesus. Later you might help your own kids. But right now, you can tell your friends or unbelieving family members about how Jesus loves them.

Where did you first learn about Jesus?

Jesus, please help me to live for you and to tell others about how you love them.

You can read about what Paul taught Timothy in 2 Timothy 1:5–14.

DAY 44

GOD HEARS

We will stand in your presence . . . and will cry out to you in our distress.

2 CHRONICLES 20:9

Did you know grasshoppers could be deadly pests?

For five years in the late 1800s, grasshoppers descended on farms in Minnesota and destroyed crops. Farmers tried trapping the grasshoppers in tar and burning their fields to kill the eggs. Desperate, the people asked for a statewide day of prayer in April so they could seek God's help together. The governor set aside a day. Soon after the group prayer, the weather warmed up and the eggs started to come to life. But then four days later freezing temperatures killed the larvae. Thanks to answered prayer, the farmers would harvest their crops.

Prayer was also behind the saving of God's people during the reign of King Jehoshaphat (2 Chronicles 20:1–29). When the king learned a vast army was coming against the Israelites to destroy them, he called God's people to

pray and fast. The people cried out to God. God heard and saved them.

God rescued His people from the invading armies, and He hears you when you pray. Whatever your concern—an argument with a friend or a problem at school—you can ask God for help. Nothing is too hard for Him.

What are you worried about?

Dear God, I need help with _____.
Thank you for hearing my prayer.

You can read about King Jehoshaphat's prayer and God's answer in 2 Chronicles 20:5–12, 15.

DAY  45

DELIGHT IN THE BOOK

Keep this Book of the Law always on your lips;
meditate on it day and night.

JOSHUA 1:8

Do you love books? What's your favorite? Do you—or perhaps your mom or dad—have a stack of books on a bedside table waiting to be read? There's a Japanese word for that. It's *tsundoku.*

Books can offer a fun escape to a different time or place. They can teach us new skills or ideas. Some books do both. The idea that we can find enjoyment and help in a book is even more true for the Bible.

When Joshua became the new leader of Israel, he needed encouragement. As he prepared to lead the Israelites into the promised land, God assured him that He'd be with him. But God also told him to "meditate on [Scripture] day and night, so that you may be careful to do everything written in it" (Joshua 1:8). When he did, Joshua would learn all about God and what He wanted him to do.

The Bible is a book of true stories about people long ago, faraway places, and wisdom for living. But most of all it's a book that teaches us all about our loving God. He wants you to love and follow Him. One of the best ways to learn how to do that is to read His book, the Bible.

What's your favorite part or story of the Bible?

God, I want to learn all about you. Help me to delight in your book.

You can read about Joshua in Joshua 1:1–9.

DAY 46

DO WHAT'S RIGHT

Hate what is evil; cling to what is good.

ROMANS 12:9

Track star Jesse Owens was a courageous man of faith. During the 1936 Olympic Games in Berlin, Owens, an African American on the US team, received four gold medals in the presence of hate-filled Nazis and their leader, Hitler. While there, he befriended fellow athlete Luz Long, a German. Owens's simple act of living out his faith impacted Long's life. Later, Long wrote to Owens: "That hour in Berlin when I first spoke to you, when you had your knee upon the ground, I knew you were in prayer. . . . I think I might believe in God."

Owens showed how believers can live out the apostle Paul's reminder to "hate what is evil" and be "devoted to one another in love" (Romans 12:9–10). Though he could have responded to the evil around him with hate, Owens chose to live by faith and be kind to a man who would later become his friend and consider belief in God.

When we pray, God helps us to "live in harmony with one another" (v. 16).

If you believe in Jesus and talk to Him in prayer, He'll help you to do what's right and good—and to love even unlovable people.

Who do you have trouble loving?

Dear Jesus, help me to do what's right.

You can read about love in action in Romans 12:9–21.

DAY 47

KEEP SMILING!

A cheerful heart is good medicine.

PROVERBS 17:22

No matter where she is, Marcia likes to smile at people. It's her way of being kind to people who might need to see a friendly face. Most of the time, they smile back. But when she had to wear a face mask during COVID, she realized people could no longer see her smile. She kept smiling anyway, hoping they would see in her eyes that she was smiling.

Science supports that idea. The muscles for the corners of the mouth and the ones that make the eyes crinkle can work together. It's called a *Duchenne* smile, and it has been described as "smiling with the eyes."

The book of Proverbs says, "a cheerful look brings joy to the heart" (15:30 NLT) and "a cheerful heart is good medicine" (17:22). Quite often, the smiles of God's children come from the joy we receive from the Holy Spirit inside us. It's a gift from God that spills out into our lives

as we encourage people. Even when we're having a hard time, our joy can still shine through.

Keep smiling. God loves you!

Why do you think it's important to smile?

I love you, God. Help me to show your love through my smile.

You can read about joy in Proverbs 15:13–15, 30.

DAY 48

PRAYER EGGS

Though it linger, wait for it; it will certainly come and will not delay.

HABAKKUK 2:3

Just outside Ashley's kitchen window, a robin built her nest under the eaves of her family's patio roof. Ashley loved watching the busy robin as it worked on the nest and then settled down to incubate the eggs. Each morning she checked their progress; but each morning, there was nothing. Robin eggs take two weeks to hatch.

It was hard for Ashley to wait—not only for the birds to hatch but for lots of things. And that included her prayers. Sometimes it seemed to take forever for God to answer. She had to learn the truth that "prayers, like eggs, don't hatch as soon as we lay them."

The prophet Habakkuk also wrestled with waiting in prayer. God revealed to the prophet that Babylon, an enemy of God's people, was about to conquer and mistreat them. Frustrated by the situation and by God's silence,

Habakkuk decided to "stand at my watch and station myself on the ramparts," to see what God would say to him (Habakkuk 2:1). God replied that Habakkuk was to wait for the "appointed time" (v. 3). What God didn't mention is that the "appointed time" when Babylon would fall was six decades away, creating a long gap between God's promise and its fulfillment.

Like eggs, prayers often don't hatch immediately. Sometimes, we have to wait. But you can trust that God hears and will provide.

What is the hardest thing about waiting?

God, I don't like waiting. Help me to trust that you will answer my prayer.

You can read about God's answer to Habakkuk in Habakkuk 2:1–3.

IN NEED OF RESCUE

A Samaritan, as he traveled, came where the man was; and when he saw him, he took pity on him.

LUKE 10:33

A teenager named Aldi was working alone on a fishing hut anchored off an island in Indonesia. Suddenly, heavy winds knocked the hut off its mooring and sent it out to sea. For forty-nine days, Aldi drifted in the ocean. Every time he spotted a ship, he turned on his lamp to get their attention. About ten ships passed the malnourished teen before he was rescued.

Jesus told a parable to a law expert about someone who needed to be rescued. Two men—first a priest and then a Levite—saw an injured man as they were traveling. But rather than help him, they "passed by on the other side" (Luke 10:31–32). We don't know why. Both were religious men. Perhaps they thought it was too dangerous. Or they didn't want to break Jewish laws about touching dead bodies. But a Samaritan—who was hated by the

Jews—did what was right. He saw the man in need and took care of him.

Jesus concluded His teaching with the command that His followers (that means you) should "go and do likewise" (v. 37). God wants us to reach out in love to help others.

Why is it sometimes good to be cautious before helping someone?

Dear God, help me to be willing to help others.

You can read this parable in Luke 10:30–37.

DAY 50

WILL THEY NOTICE?

They hid from the LORD God among the trees of the garden.

GENESIS 3:8

Ten-year-old Britney knew she shouldn't have done it. She knew it was wrong. But all her friends were doing it. As her mom sat down to talk with her, Britney kept her eyes glued to her lap. She thought that if her mom couldn't see her eyes, she wouldn't see her guilt and perhaps Britney could avoid the conversation and the consequences.

Her mom couldn't approve of Britney's actions, and they needed to talk about it, but the loving mom didn't want anything to come between them. She wanted her daughter to look at her and see how much she loved her and was eager to forgive! In that moment, her mom caught a glimmer of how God might have felt when Adam and Eve broke His trust in the garden of Eden. Realizing their guilt, they tried to hide from God. But He could "see" them as plainly as Britney's mom could see her.

When you realize you've done something wrong, what do you do? Do you try to hide it or hope no one will notice? Although God will hold you accountable, He wants you to come to Him because He loves you and offers forgiveness through Jesus Christ.

What do you need to ask forgiveness for right now?

God, thank you for forgiving me when I mess up.

You can read about Adam and Eve's sin and God's response in Genesis 3:1–10.

BIG ENOUGH

Let the little children come to me, and do not hinder them, for the kingdom of God belongs to such as these.

LUKE 18:16

The little girl ran to the roller coaster line and stood with her back against the height-requirement sign. Was she big enough to ride? She squealed with joy when her head exceeded the mark. So much of life is about being "big" enough, isn't it? To move from car seat to seat belt and from the back seat to the front. To be old enough to drive.

Perhaps like that young girl, you can't wait to grow up. In New Testament times, children were loved but not highly valued until they "became of age" and could contribute to the home and enter the synagogue with adult privileges. Jesus shattered the standards of His day by welcoming the poor, the sick, and even children.

The Gospels tell of parents bringing little children to Jesus so He could bless and pray for them. The disciples scolded the parents. But Jesus told the disciples to let them come. He welcomed the children and showed how He valued them. He even challenged the adults to become like children themselves—to embrace their need for Him in order to know Him. Jesus gladly welcomes all who come to Him.

What can't you wait to be old enough to do?

Jesus, thank you for loving kids like me.

You can read about Jesus welcoming children in Luke 18:15–17.

THE DOOR

All this is from God, who reconciled us to himself through Christ and gave us the ministry of reconciliation.

2 CORINTHIANS 5:18

Inside St. Patrick's Cathedral in Dublin, Ireland, there's a door that tells a story. Long, long ago in 1492, two families, the Butlers and the FitzGeralds, began fighting over a job. The fight got out of control, and the Butlers took shelter in the cathedral. When the FitzGeralds came to ask for a truce, the Butlers were afraid to open the door. So, the FitzGeralds cut a hole in it, and their leader offered his hand in peace. The two families then reconciled—made peace—and became friends.

The apostle Paul wrote about God's door of peacemaking in his letter to the church in Corinth. Because of His never-ending love, God exchanged our broken relationship with Him for a restored relationship through Jesus's death on the cross. Because of our sin, we were far away from God, but in His mercy He doesn't count our sins against us. "God made [Jesus] who had no sin to be sin for us," so that in Him we could be at peace with God (2 Corinthians 5:21).

When we accept God's offer of salvation, we know that one day we'll be with Him! There's no better reason to tell others about Him.

What do you think is the best thing about God?

Jesus, thank you for dying for me and making a way for me to be with you forever!

You can read about what it means to be reconciled or forgiven in 2 Corinthians 5:14–21.

DAY 53

OPEN ARMS

In my distress I called to the LORD. . . .
My cry came to his ears.

2 SAMUEL 22:7

Saydee and his family have an "open arms and open home" philosophy. People are always welcome in their home, "especially those who are in distress," he says. That's the kind of home he had growing up in Liberia with his nine siblings. Their parents always welcomed others into their family.

He says, "We grew up as a community. We loved one another. Everybody was responsible for everybody. My dad taught us to love each other, care for each other, protect each other."

When King David needed help, he found this type of loving care in God. God had been a refuge for him throughout his life. He recalled, "In my distress I called to the LORD; I called out to my God. From his temple he heard my voice; my cry came to his ears" (2 Samuel 22:7). God

delivered David from his enemies, including King Saul, many times.

No matter your problem, God welcomes you to run to Him to find the help you need. No problem is too big or too small for Him! His arms are always open.

What concern do you need to bring to God right now?

God, I need help with _____.

You can read about how God was David's refuge in 2 Samuel 22:1–7, 17–20.

54

WALK LIKE A WARRIOR

When the angel of the LORD appeared to Gideon, he said, "The LORD is with you, mighty warrior."

JUDGES 6:12

Eighteen-year-old Emma talks about Jesus on social media, even though bullies criticize her joy and love for Christ. Some attack her with remarks about how she looks. Others mock her because she loves God. Though the unkind words cut deep into Emma's heart, she keeps spreading the gospel with bold faith and love for Jesus and others.

Sometimes, though, she's tempted to believe the negative things people say about her. When that happens, she asks God for help, prays for those who bully her, and remembers what God says about her in the Bible—that she's valuable and loved. Then she continues with the courage and confidence God provides.

Gideon faced fierce bullies—the Midianites. Though God called him a "mighty warrior," Gideon struggled to let go of his doubts and insecurities (Judges 6:12). More than once, he questioned the Lord's presence and his own ability to lead, but eventually he believed that God would strengthen and equip Him for the fight.

When you trust God, you can show by the way you live that you believe what He says about you is true. Even when others' comments may tempt you to doubt your worth, God fights on your behalf. He'll help you to walk like a mighty warrior. He thinks you're special!

Why is it best to want to please
God rather than people?

Dear God, help me to believe that I am lovable and loved.

You can read about Gideon in Judges 6:1, 11–16.

RUNNING FOR THE PRIZE

Run in such a way as to get the prize.

1 CORINTHIANS 9:24

Eric Liddell was a winning athlete. When he ran, he focused on being the very best runner he could be. In competition, he broke world records, and he won an Olympic gold medal and a bronze medal too! But he loved God even more than running. In a movie about his life, *Chariots of Fire*, Eric said, "I believe that God made me for a purpose . . . but He also made me fast. And when I run, I feel His pleasure."

After the Olympics, Eric moved to China to be a missionary teacher. Eric spent the rest of his life focused on a new goal: showing people just how much Jesus loves them.

Was training for running or missionary work easy? No way. I'm sure Eric had to say no to some fun things so he could train. His missionary "race" was hard, but he loved God and wanted everyone know the good news of Jesus.

The apostle Paul asked his readers to follow his example and "run in such a way as to get the prize" (1 Corinthians 9:24). Like Eric, your running—the way you live your life—might mean saying no to some things. It might mean stopping when you feel like arguing with your mom.

Running the race to win the ultimate prize—a life that honors God—begins with doing what's right. God wants you to run with the goal of telling and showing others His love. That's the best reason to run!

What can you do to live for God?

Dear God, I want to do what's right. Help me, please.

You can read about living for God
in 1 Corinthians 9:24–27.

JESUS SEES YOU

For the Son of Man came to seek and to save the lost.

LUKE 19:10

Lisa was in the middle of the crowd at a motorcycle show but could barely see the riders perform their tricks. So she stood on her tiptoes. Glancing around, she spied three kids perched in a nearby tree. Like her, they probably couldn't get to the front of the crowd to see the action.

Someone in the Bible also climbed a tree for a better view. It was Zacchaeus, a hated tax collector. Tax collectors were considered traitors because they worked for the hated Roman government collecting taxes from other Jews. What's worse, they often demanded extra money for themselves.

One day as Jesus passed through Jericho, Zacchaeus longed to see Him but was unable to see over the crowd. So he climbed into a sycamore tree. It was there, on the outskirts of the crowd, that Jesus searched out the tax collector and invited himself to be a guest at Zacchaeus's home.

Zacchaeus's story reminds us that Jesus came to "seek and to save the lost," offering His friendship and the gift of salvation (Luke 19:9–10). Even if you feel left out or unseen, Jesus sees you and wants to spend time with you.

What's your favorite part of Zacchaeus's story?

Dear Jesus, thank you for seeing and loving me.

You can read about Zacchaeus in Luke 19:1–10.

ON OUR HEARTS

These commandments . . . are to be on your hearts.
Impress them on your children.

DEUTERONOMY 6:6–7

After a little girl had trouble in school, her dad began to teach her a pledge to recite each morning before school: "I thank God for waking me up today. I am going to school so I can learn . . . and be the leader that God has created me to be." The father hoped to help his daughter apply herself and deal with life's challenges.

By helping his daughter to learn this pledge, the father is doing something similar to what God taught the Israelites in the desert: "These commandments . . . are to be on your hearts. Impress them on your children" (Deuteronomy 6:6–7).

After wandering in the wilderness for forty years, the Israelites were about to enter the new land God had promised to them. God knew the journey wouldn't be easy for them unless they kept their focus on Him. So, through Moses,

He urged them to remember and be obedient to Him. God told the people to help their children know and love God by talking about His commandments "when you sit at home and when you walk along the road, when you lie down and when you get up" (v. 7).

When you're young, it's a great time to memorize Scripture and to learn more about God.

What Scripture passage would you like to memorize?

Dear God, help me to want to get to know you.

You can read about what God wanted the Israelites and what He wants you to understand in Deuteronomy 6:4–9.

DAY 58

LIVING WATER

Let anyone who is thirsty come to me and drink.

JOHN 7:37

Did you enjoy running through a sprinkler when you were younger? Perhaps you still do. There's nothing like cooling off in cold water on a hot day!

You can see that kind of joy in the video Tom and Mark share of a group of kids laughing and dancing in the refreshing water of an open shower—their first ever. The men work with local churches in Haiti to install water filtration systems on wells. These filters help prevent diseases connected to contaminated water. Access to clean, fresh water gives the people hope for their future.

One day when Jesus was tired and thirsty, He asked a Samaritan woman for a drink (John 4:4–8). As they talked, Jesus offered her "living water"—the most refreshing water ever. Later, Jesus explained the source of this living water: "Let anyone who is thirsty come to me and drink" (7:37). Whoever believed in Him would have "rivers of living water [flowing] from within them" (v. 38). He was talking about the Holy Spirit.

When we receive Jesus as our Savior, He gives us the Spirit. Like living water, the Spirit lives inside us and guides us and gives us joy.

What's the best part of having the Holy Spirit inside you?

Dear God, thank you for being with me every day.

You can read about living water in John 4:4–14.

DAY 59

BETRAYED

Even my close friend, someone I trusted, one who shared my bread, has turned against me.

PSALM 41:9

Have you heard of Leonardo da Vinci, an artist who lived over five hundred years ago? He's famous for his drawings and scientific discoveries, but especially for his painting *The Last Supper*.

This painting pictures the final meal Jesus ate with His disciples, which we learn about in the Gospels—Matthew, Mark, Luke, and John. It shows the disciples' confusion when Jesus says, "One of you is going to betray me" (John 13:21). The disciples wondered who the betrayer might be—while Judas quietly slipped out into the night to sell out Jesus.

Betrayed. Jesus's pain is clear in His words, "He who shared my bread has turned against me" (v. 18). A friend close enough to share a meal used that connection to harm Jesus.

Has a friend turned against you or said untrue things about you? It really hurts. Psalm 41:9, which Jesus quoted to indicate His betrayer was with him during the meal, offers hope. After David poured out his anguish at a close friend's lies, he found comfort in God's love and presence.

When friends disappoint you, you can turn to God. He "will never leave you nor forsake you" (Joshua 1:5).

How does it help to know Jesus went through some of the same things you're going through?

Dear Jesus, thank you for loving and never leaving me.

You can read about Jesus's betrayal in
John 13:18–22 and Psalm 41:9.

DAY 60

PERSPECTIVE FROM ABOVE

I will not yield my glory to another.

ISAIAH 48:11

When Peter Welch was a kid in the 1970s, using a metal detector was just a hobby. But since 1990, he's been leading people from around the world on metal-detecting trips. They've made thousands of discoveries, including swords, ancient jewelry, and coins. They use Google Earth to show them where roads, buildings, and other structures may have been centuries ago. Peter says, "To have a perspective from above opens a whole new world."

God's people in Isaiah's day needed "a perspective from above." They took pride in being His people, yet they disobeyed God and refused to stop worshiping idols. Despite their rebellion, God would rescue them from captivity to Babylon. Why? "For my own sake, . . . I will not yield my glory to another" (Isaiah 48:11). God's perspective from above is that life is for His praise and purpose—not ours.

Our focus is to be on Him and His plans and telling others about Him.

If you love and want to serve God, a whole new world will open for you. You'll discover new things about God and the life He has uniquely designed for you. He'll teach you what is good for you and what path you should follow.

What is one thing you can do to
change your perspective?

Dear God, help me to devote my life to you.

You can read about God's perspective
in Isaiah 48:5–11, 17.

DAY 61

LIFE CHANGES

Put on the new self, created to be like God in true righteousness and holiness.

EPHESIANS 4:24

Stephen grew up in a rough part of East London and got into crime by the age of ten. He said, "If everyone's selling drugs and doing robberies and fraud, then you're going to get involved. It's just a way of life." But when he was twenty, he had a dream that changed him: "I heard God saying, 'Stephen, you're going to prison for murder.'"

Stephen's dream served as a warning, and he turned to God and received Jesus as his Savior. The Holy Spirit transformed his life. He set up an organization that teaches inner-city kids discipline, morality, and respect through sports. He credits God with his success as he prays with and trains the kids.

When you love Jesus and decide not to do the things you know are wrong, you're choosing a new way of life, a "new self" that's created to be like God. You're in the process of becoming more like God through His Holy Spirit inside you. It isn't always easy to do the right thing, but you can trust Him to help you as you grow.

What do you think it means to put on a "new self"?

Dear God, please help me to be more like Jesus.

You can read about what it means to have a new self in Ephesians 4:20–24.

DAY 62

WANDERING OFF

Rejoice with me; I have found my lost sheep.

LUKE 15:6

Did you know cows tend to wander while grazing? A cow will keep moving, always looking for greener pastures. Near the edge of the property, the cow might discover some fresh grass under a shade tree. Just beyond a broken-down part of the fence might be a tasty clump of foliage. Then the cow might push far beyond the fence and out to the road. It slowly nibbles its way into being lost.

Cows aren't the only ones that roam. Sheep wander too. But people probably have the biggest tendency of all to stray. Perhaps that's one reason God compares us to sheep in the Bible. It can be easy to meander and "nibble our way" through bad choices, especially when we get older.

In the parable of the lost sheep, the shepherd left his other sheep behind to search for the wandering one. When he found it, he celebrated (Luke 15:1–7). That's how happy

God is when someone who has strayed turns back to Him. Jesus said, "Rejoice with me; I have found my lost sheep" (v. 6). God sent us a Savior to rescue us and bring us home. If we stay close to Him, we're less likely to roam.

What's one way you can stay close to God?

Dear God, help me to make wise choices now and as I get older.

You can read the parable of the lost sheep in Luke 15:1–7.

DAY 63

ORDINARY

People look at the outward appearance,
but the LORD looks at the heart.

1 SAMUEL 16:7

In the late 1700s, William Carey grew up in a poor family in England and was often sick. His future didn't look bright. But God had plans for him. He moved to India, where he told the people living there about Jesus and translated the Bible into several Indian languages. He loved God and people and accomplished many good things.

David, Jesse's son, was an ordinary young man, the youngest in his family. He was a shepherd on the hills of Bethlehem. Yet God saw David's heart and had a plan for him. King Saul had been rejected by God for disobedience, so God called the prophet Samuel to anoint a different king, one of Jesse's sons.

When Samuel saw the oldest son, handsome Eliab, he thought, "Surely the LORD's anointed stands here before the LORD" (1 Samuel 16:6). But God's strategy to select a king was much different from Samuel's. In fact, God said no to each of Jesse's sons—except the youngest. Selecting David as king didn't seem to be a wise move on God's part. What would a young shepherd have to offer? A lot! David unified his country Israel and much more! And from his family tree, Jesus was born.

God has plans for you, too, if you're willing.

Why is it good to know that God uses ordinary people to accomplish good things?

Dear God, I'm a normal girl who wants to do great things for you. Guide me, please.

You can read about Samuel's decision in 1 Samuel 16:1–7.

DAY 64

SMALL BUT MIGHTY

We are God's handiwork, created in Christ Jesus to do good works.

EPHESIANS 2:10

Sometimes late at night in North America's harsh Sonoran Desert, you can hear a faint, high-pitched howl. But you probably wouldn't suspect the source of the sound—the small grasshopper mouse, howling at the moon to establish its territory.

This unique rodent (called the "werewolf mouse") is also carnivorous. In fact, it preys on creatures few would dare mess with, such as the scorpion. But the werewolf mouse is uniquely equipped for that battle. It not only has a resistance to scorpion venom, but it can also change the toxins into a painkiller!

This mighty little mouse seems custom-made to survive and even thrive in the desert. As Paul explains in Ephesians 2:10, that kind of craftsmanship represents God's designs for His people as well. Each of us is "God's handiwork," uniquely equipped to serve Him. Right now, you have so much to offer. And as you grow into the woman God has designed you to be, you can share God's hope and joy—because He lives and works in you!

If the future feels scary, take courage. You may be young, but God can use you to do mighty things.

What creature do you find most amazing?

Dear God, help me as I grow to discover what I can do for you.

You can read about God's love for you in Ephesians 2:4–10.

NAMED BY GOD

"Don't call me Naomi," she told them. "Call me Mara,
because the Almighty has made my life very bitter."
RUTH 1:20

Riptide. Batgirl. Jumpstart. Those are some of the names
given to counselors at the summer camp Lisa's family
attends every year. The nicknames usually come from an
embarrassing incident, a funny habit, or a favorite hobby.

Nicknames aren't limited to camp—we even find them
in the Bible. For example, Jesus calls the apostles James
and John the "sons of thunder" (Mark 3:17). It's rare in
Scripture for someone to give themselves a nickname, yet
it happens when Naomi asks people to call her "Mara,"
which means "bitterness" (Ruth 1:20). Because her husband and sons had died, she felt God had made her life
bitter.

But Naomi's nickname didn't stick because those losses
were not the end of her story. In her sorrow, God had
blessed her with a loving daughter-in-law, Ruth, who

eventually remarried and had a son, creating a new family for Naomi.

Do you have a nickname you don't like or a negative name you've given yourself? Remember, those names are not the end of your story. God has given you the name of "loved one" (Romans 9:25). He cares for you and will help you through hard times.

What positive nickname can you give yourself?

Dear God, help me to see myself as you
see me: loved and uniquely made.

You can read about Naomi in Ruth 1:19–22.

BORROWED SHOES

Serve one another humbly in love.

GALATIANS 5:13

When his family fled their home during a California wildfire, Gabe, a high school senior, missed the state-qualifying cross-country race he'd been training for. Missing that race meant he couldn't compete at the state meet, the conclusion of his four-year running career.

The state athletics board gave Gabe another chance. He'd have to run a qualifying time by himself on a rival high school's track. But all Gabe had were "street shoes," because his running shoes had been destroyed in the fire. When he arrived, Gabe was surprised to see his competitors had shown up to help. They gave him running shoes, and then they ran alongside him so he could keep the pace necessary to be entered in the state meet.

Those students didn't have to help Gabe. Their actions were an example of what the apostle Paul taught when he urged us to display the fruit of the Spirit in our lives—to "serve one another humbly in love" and to demonstrate "kindness" and "goodness" (Galatians 5:13, 22).

If you ask God to help you to be kind, the Holy Spirit will give you opportunities to show love to others.

How can you be kind to someone today?

Dear God, help me to show kindness.

You can read about what it means to be led by the Spirit in Galatians 5:13–26.

DAY 67

DON'T BE DECEIVED!

[The devil] is a liar and the father of lies.

JOHN 8:44

Can you think of anything that's pretty but dangerous? That describes the spotted lanternfly. It's a pretty insect with speckled outer wings and a splotch of bright red on its inner wings. But its beauty is deceptive. This bug spreads quickly and is a danger, especially to fruit growers. It eats the insides of woody plants, including cherry and other fruit trees. It leaves a sticky goo that leads to mold that can kill trees or leave them with little energy to grow fruit.

In the story of Adam and Eve, we read of a far worse menace. The serpent, Satan, tricked them into disobeying God and eating the forbidden fruit so they would "be like God" (Genesis 3:5). But why would they listen to a serpent? The Bible suggests he was created beautiful. Yet he fell by the same temptation he used to trap Eve: "I will make myself like [God]" (Isaiah 14:14).

Any beauty Satan has is used to deceive. His aim is to keep us from growing in our faith. But God is far more powerful! He loves us and wants us to trust in Him. He speaks truth, not lies.

Why is it good that God is much more powerful than Satan or any person on earth?

Jesus, I'm so glad I can bring any problem, fear, or question to you.

You can read about the temptation of Adam and Eve in Genesis 3:1–7.

BRING WHAT YOU HAVE

"Bring them here to me," [Jesus] said.

MATTHEW 14:18

"Stone Soup" is the story of a hungry man who came to a village where no one had any food to spare. So, he put a stone and water in a pot over a fire. The villagers watched as he began to stir his "soup." Eventually, one brought a couple of potatoes to add to the pot; another brought a few carrots. One added an onion, another a handful of barley. A farmer donated some milk. Eventually, the "stone soup" became a tasty chowder.

That tale shows the value of sharing, but it also reminds us to use our talents and abilities, even if they seem small or insignificant, to help others. In John 6 we read of a boy who appeared to be the only person in a huge crowd who brought food. Jesus's disciples had little use for the boy's lunch. It was only five little loaves and two fish. But Jesus increased it and fed thousands of hungry people!

Someone said, "You don't have to feed the five thousand. You just have to bring your loaves and fishes." Just as Jesus took one boy's meal and multiplied it far beyond anyone's imagination, Jesus wants you to give yourself and what you have to Him. He will use you to bless others—if not now, later.

What could you give right now to be used by Jesus?

Dear Jesus, I want to be used by You to help others. Help me to see needs that I can help with.

You can read about how Jesus used a boy's lunch to feed over five thousand people in John 6:4–14.

DAY **69**

THE MAKER OF THE MOON

*[The Lord said,] "I will be their God
and they will be my people."*

JEREMIAH 31:33

In July 1969, Neil Armstrong stepped onto the moon's surface and said, "That's one small step for man, one giant leap for mankind." He was the first man to walk on the moon. Other space travelers followed, including the commander of the last Apollo mission, Gene Cernan. He gazed at the earth and felt that "it was just too beautiful to happen by accident. . . . There has to be somebody bigger than you and bigger than me." From their unique view in deep space, these men understood their smallness in comparison to the vast universe.

The prophet Jeremiah was amazed that God, the Maker of all, promised His people love, forgiveness, and hope through friendship with Him (Jeremiah 31:33–34). He described God as He who "appoints the sun to shine by day, who decrees the moon and stars to shine by night"

(v. 35). Yet this mighty God loves us and wants us to get to know and love Him.

We'll never finish exploring the vastness of the heavens and depths of the earth. But you can be amazed at the complexity of the universe and trust the maker of the moon and all creation. He loves you!

What's the most amazing thing about the universe?

Dear God, thank you for the beautiful world you created. You're awesome!

You can read about our mighty Creator in Jeremiah 31:33–37.

DAY 70

BEING CONTENT

Godliness with contentment is great gain.

1 TIMOTHY 6:6

Lindsay's grandparents grew up during the Great Depression in the 1930s, so they knew what it meant to go without lots of things. As a result, they became hardworking adults who were grateful for what they had. They gave time, talent, and money to their church and the needy. They used their money wisely and gave cheerfully.

As believers in Jesus, Lindsay's grandparents took to heart the apostle Paul's warning that those whose goal is to get rich can be tempted to do unwise and harmful things. Paul gave this advice to Timothy, the young pastor in the wealthy city of Ephesus. "The love of money is a root of all kinds of evil," he warned. "Some people, eager for money, have wandered from the faith and pierced themselves with many griefs" (1 Timothy 6:10).

What's the antidote to greed? It's being content with what you have. By learning about and loving God above all, He becomes your chief delight. Being thankful for all He's done and given you helps you to appreciate what you have so that as you grow, you can help and give to others!

What are you grateful for?

Dear God, help me to be content with what I have.

You can read about contentment in 1 Timothy 6:6–10.

DAY 71

STRONG AND COURAGEOUS

As I was with Moses, so I will be with you;
I will never leave you nor forsake you.

JOSHUA 1:5

Each night, as Ariana closed her eyes, she heard the creaking of the wooden house. Then the bats in the attic became active. Her mom had put a night-light in her room, but she was still afraid. One night Ariana's dad posted a Bible verse on the footboard of her bed: "Be strong and courageous. Do not be afraid; . . . for the Lord your God will be with you" (Joshua 1:9). Ariana read those words each night until she went away to college.

After Joshua became the new leader of the Israelites, God told Joshua and the people to "be strong and courageous." They were afraid as they faced an uncertain future, but God told them, "As I was with Moses, so I will be with you; I will never leave you nor forsake you" (Joshua 1:5).

It's natural to have fears, but it's not good to be afraid all the time. Just as God encouraged His people long

ago, you too can be strong and courageous because God promises to be with you always. You can give your concerns to Him in prayer.

What are you afraid of?

Dear God, please help me not to be afraid of _____.

You can read about how God encouraged
Joshua and the Israelites in Joshua 1:1–9.

DAY 72

INSIDE THE FIRE

*I see four men walking around in the fire,
unbound and unharmed.*

DANIEL 3:25

A wildfire in Spain scorched nearly fifty thousand acres of woodland. However, in the middle of the devastation, a group of nearly one thousand cypress trees remained standing. The trees' ability to retain water had allowed them to survive the fire.

During King Nebuchadnezzar's reign in Babylon, three friends survived the flames of the king's anger. Shadrach, Meshach, and Abednego refused to worship a statue the king created, saying, "If we are thrown into the blazing furnace, the God we serve is able to deliver us from it" (Daniel 3:17). Enraged, the ruler cranked up the heat seven times hotter than normal.

The soldiers who tossed the men into the blaze were burned up, yet Shadrach, Meshach, and Abednego walked around inside the flames "unbound and unharmed" (v. 25).

Someone else was also in the furnace—a fourth man who looked "like a son of the gods" (v. 25)—an angel or perhaps even Christ.

Jesus is with you when you face troubles. When someone pushes you to do something you know is wrong, you don't have to be afraid to say no. God is with you. He'll give you the strength to stay faithful to Him and to do what's right.

What difficult time have you had to face?

Jesus, please help me to know you are with me even during trouble.

You can read about how God delivered three friends from a fiery furnace in Daniel 3:12–28.

DAY 73

PERFECTLY PLACED

Where were you when I laid the earth's foundation?

JOB 38:4

Did you know Earth is exactly the right distance from the sun to benefit from its heat? A little closer and all the water would evaporate, as on Venus. Only a bit farther away and everything would freeze like it does on Mars. Earth is also just the right size to generate the right amount of gravity. Less would make everything weightless like on our moon, while more gravity would trap poisonous gases that suffocate life as on Jupiter.

All these details about our world point to an intelligent Designer. We catch a glimpse of His complex craftsmanship when God speaks to Job about things we don't understand. "Where were you when I laid the earth's foundation?" God asks. "Who marked off its dimensions? Surely you know! Who stretched a measuring line across it? On what were its footings set, or who laid its cornerstone?" (Job 38:4–6).

When you think about the vastness of creation, it can make your head spin. And what's even more amazing is that God created this world for us because He loves us and wants us to know and trust Him. Doesn't that make you want to sing?

What do you think is the most wonderful thing about Earth?

Dear God, thank you for the awesome world you made!

You can read about God's creative power in Job 38:4–11.

DAY **74**

A GREEN PEN

Whoever heeds life-giving correction
will be at home among the wise.

PROVERBS 15:31

Did you ever get a paper back from a teacher all marked in red? Ugh! Cindy's dad was an editor. He looked for mistakes but also tried to make the writing clear and to the point. He used a green pen for his corrections, rather than a red one. He thought a green pen was "friendlier," while slashes of red might be jarring to a new or less confident writer. His goal was to gently point out a better way.

When Jesus corrected people, He did so in love. Sometimes He rebuked people harshly yet still for their benefit. In the case of His friend Martha, a gentle correction was all she needed (Luke 10:38–42). While some people responded poorly, Martha remained one of His dearest friends.

No one likes to be corrected. Yet the book of Proverbs tells us that listening to "life-giving correction" is a sign of wisdom and understanding (15:31–32). God's loving correction helps us to make better decisions and follow Him more closely. That's why He gave us parents and other trusted adults to guide us in the right way. If you listen to and follow loving correction, God will help you to grow to be a wise and godly woman.

How has someone's correction helped
you to make good decisions?

*God, I don't like to be corrected. But
I know I sometimes need it.*

You can read about Martha's
correction in Luke 10:38–42.

DAY 75

MORNING MIST

I have swept away your offenses . . .
like the morning mist.

ISAIAH 44:22

One morning Jenny dragged herself to the nearby pond. She plopped down on an overturned boat and watched as a gentle breeze chased a layer of mist across the water's surface. Wisps of fog circled and swirled. Before long, the sunlight cut through the clouds and the mist disappeared.

Jenny remembered the verse she'd just read: "I have swept away your offenses like a cloud, your sins like the morning mist" (Isaiah 44:22). She went to the pond because she'd been bothered by some unkind things she'd said and done. Although she'd confessed, she wondered if God would forgive her when she kept repeating the same sins.

That morning, Jenny knew the answer was yes. Through the prophet Isaiah, God showed grace to the Israelites when they struggled with their ongoing problem of idol worship. Although He wanted them to stop, God also invited them to return to Him, saying, "I have made you. . . . I will not forget you" (v. 21).

You may not fully understand God's forgiveness, but if you're His child you can be certain God loves you and has forgiven you. Jesus died for your sins so you can be free. Pray and ask for His forgiveness and help to do better. He hears and forgives.

What sin do you need forgiveness for?

Dear God, I need help with _____.

You can read about God's forgiveness
in Isaiah 44:9–11, 21–23.

DAY 76

IN THE GARDEN

Mary Magdalene went to the disciples with the news:
"I have seen the Lord!"

JOHN 20:18

Alyson's dad loved to sing old hymns. One of his favorites was "In the Garden." The chorus is simple: "And He walks with me, and He talks with me, and He tells me I am His own, and the joy we share as we tarry there, none other has ever known." That song brought joy to her dad . . . and to Alyson.

The hymn writer wrote this song in the spring of 1912 after reading John 20. "As I read it that day, I seemed to be part of the scene. I became a silent witness to that dramatic moment in Mary's life when she knelt before her Lord and cried, '[Teacher].'"

On the third day after Jesus was buried, Mary Magdalene wept near His empty tomb. There she met a man who asked why she was crying. She thought He was the gardener, but He was the risen Savior—Jesus! Her sorrow turned to joy, and she ran to tell the disciples, "I have seen the Lord!" (John 20:18).

Jesus is risen! He's now in heaven with the Father, but He hasn't left us on our own. Believers in Christ have His Spirit inside us, and through Him, we have the joy of knowing He's with us. We are "His own."

What do you think it will be like to meet Jesus?

Jesus, I'm so glad you arose and that one day I'll be with you!

You can read about Mary's encounter with Jesus in John 20:11–18.

DAY 77

GOD COMFORTS YOU

[God] comforts us in all our troubles, so that we can comfort those in any trouble.

2 CORINTHIANS 1:4

Radamenes was a sick little kitten when his owner dropped him off at an animal shelter. He was nursed back to health and adopted by the vet. He became a full-time resident at the shelter. Now he spends his days "comforting" other cats and dogs—just out of surgery or recovering from an illness—through his warm presence and gentle purr.

That's a little like what God does for us, and what we can do for others. God cares for us when we're sick or have troubles, and He soothes us with His presence. The apostle Paul calls God "the Father of compassion and the God of all comfort" (2 Corinthians 1:3). When we're discouraged or sad, He's there for us. When we turn to Him in prayer, He comforts us. Because of what God does for us, we want to comfort others.

Are you sad or sick and need comforting? Pray. Our Savior, who suffered for us, will comfort you. He helps you through your pain so that you can help your family and friends.

What helps you to feel better when you're sad or sick?

Dear God, thank you for comforting me when I need it most.

You can read about how God comforts us in 2 Corinthians 1:3–7.

IT'S JESUS

God has chosen to make known . . . the glorious riches of this mystery, which is Christ in you, the hope of glory.

COLOSSIANS 1:27

During a TV episode of the competition *America's Got Talent*, a five-year-old girl sang with such cheer that a judge compared her to a famous child singer and dancer from the 1930s. He told her, "I think Shirley Temple is living somewhere inside of you." She replied, "Not Shirley Temple. Jesus!"

The little girl's joy came from Jesus living in her. The Bible tells us that everyone who believes and trusts in Jesus has not only the promise of eternal life with God but also Jesus's presence living in them through His Holy Spirit. In that way, our hearts become Jesus's home (Colossians 1:27).

Because Jesus lives in our hearts, we have many reasons to be grateful. The Spirit brings joy to our hearts in times of celebration but also in difficult times. He gives us hope that God is working all things together for good, even when we can't see it. And the Spirit gives us peace even when we're surrounded by troubles.

If Jesus lives in your heart, you have joy, peace, and hope. That's why you can shine out His love so others can see!

How do you feel knowing that Jesus lives inside you?

Jesus, thank you for sending your Holy Spirit to live in me!

You can read about reasons for having
joy in Colossians 1:27–29; 2:6–10.

DAY  79

OUR FATHER'S CARE

Are not two sparrows sold for a penny? Yet not one of them will fall to the ground outside your Father's care.

MATTHEW 10:29

Thwack! Elisa looked up and listened. Spotting a smudge on the windowpane, she looked out and discovered the still-alive body of a bird on her deck. She longed to help the little bird.

In Matthew 10, Jesus sent out His disciples knowing they would face danger when they tried to tell others about Him. People would oppose them and try to stop them, including governing authorities, their own families, and the devil. And so, Jesus comforted them by describing His Father's care for sparrows.

Jesus told them not to fear whatever they faced because they would never be out of their Father's care. "Are not two sparrows sold for a penny?" He asked. "Yet not one of them will fall to the ground outside your Father's care. . . .

So don't be afraid; you are worth more than many sparrows" (10:29–31).

Elisa checked on the bird throughout the day. It was alive but still there. Then, late in the evening, it was gone. She hoped it survived. Elisa cared about the bird, but God cared even more. Imagine how much He cares for you! You are worth more than anything to Him.

How does it help to know that God loves you more than any creature on the earth?

Dear God, thank you for loving me!

You can learn about God's love in Matthew 10:16–20, 26–31.

DAY 80

THE MAN IN SEAT 2D

*Be rich in good deeds, and [be] generous
and willing to share.*

1 TIMOTHY 6:18

Kelsey worked her way down the narrow airplane aisle with her eleven-month-old daughter, Lucy, and Lucy's oxygen machine. They were traveling to seek treatment for Lucy's lung disease. Just after settling into their shared seat, a flight attendant told Kelsey a passenger in first class wanted to switch seats with her. Grateful, Kelsey made her way back up the aisle to the more spacious seat, while the kind stranger made his way toward hers.

That man's action is the kind of generous living Paul encouraged. He told young pastor Timothy to instruct those in his care to "do good, to be rich in good deeds, and to be generous and willing to share" (1 Timothy 6:18). Paul knew it was tempting to rely on riches and belongings to succeed in this world. Instead, he said it's better to live a

life of generosity and service to others, becoming "rich" in good deeds, like the man from seat 2D on Kelsey's flight.

Did you know you can be generous, no matter how old you are? That includes being kind, sharing, and doing things for others. When you do, Paul says you will "take hold of the life that is truly life" (v. 19).

What good deed can you do today?

Dear God, help me to be kind and willing to share with others.

You can read about the kind of life God wants you to live in 1 Timothy 6:17–19.

DAY 81

LOOK UP!

There will be no night there.

REVELATION 21:25

When filmmaker Wylie Overstreet showed strangers a live picture of the moon as seen through his powerful telescope, they were amazed at the up-close view. To see such a glorious sight, Overstreet explained, "fills us with a sense of wonder that there's something much bigger than ourselves."

The psalmist David also marveled at God's heavenly lights. "When I consider your heavens, the work of your fingers, the moon and the stars, which you have set in place, what is mankind that you are mindful of them, human beings that you care for them?" (Psalm 8:3–4).

God loves us so much He made the sun and moon to give us light! Yet, in the end when God creates a new heaven and earth, we won't need either. Instead, God's brightness will provide all the light we'll need. "The city does not need the sun or the moon to shine on it, for the glory of

God gives it light, and the Lamb is its lamp. . . . There will be no night there" (Revelation 21:23, 25).

Can you imagine? No more sun or moon or lights of any kind—just Jesus. Until then we can see Him in His wonderful creation, including the sun, moon, and stars. When we look up, we see God.

What do you think the new heaven and earth will be like?

Thank you, God, for creating the sun, moon, and stars to give me light and to remind me of you.

You can read about how awesome God is in Psalm 8:3–4 and Revelation 21:22–25.

DAY 82

GOD IS GOOD

God's grace was so powerfully at work in them all that there were no needy persons among them.

ACTS 4:33–34

The little boy spent his early years in a children's home. Then the day came when he was adopted! Before he left with his new parents, they asked to collect his belongings. But he had none. They exchanged the clothes he was wearing for the new items they'd brought for him and left some clothing for the other children. His parents were so glad to have a little boy of their own!

A few years later, the family met a person asking for donations for families in need. Their son eagerly donated some stuffed animals and a few coins. Because he began life with little, he might have wanted to hang on to his belongings. But he didn't.

His parents thought he was generous for perhaps the same reason as the early church. God worked in the people's hearts so powerfully that they took care of each other.

They gladly sold their possessions to provide for each other's needs.

You may think you don't have much to give. But you can donate your used toys and books or give your time to help others, like offering to do something for a family in need or helping with a food drive. God can help you find ways to be generous.

If God has been good to you, how can you give of your time or things to help others?

Dear God, thank you for being generous to me. Help me to be generous to others.

You can read about the early church in Acts 4:32–35.

DAY 83

OUR REASON FOR JOY

Let Israel rejoice in their Maker; let the people of Zion be glad in their King.

PSALM 149:2

Fourteen-year-old C.J. hopped off the school bus every afternoon and danced down his driveway. His mom recorded and shared videos of C.J.'s after-school dance showing how he enjoyed life and "making people happy" with every move.

His dancing inspired others to dance with him. One day, two garbage collectors took a few minutes out of their busy work schedule to stomp, spin, and sway with C.J. This trio showed the power of sincere and infectious joy.

What's the source of unstoppable joy? The writer of Psalm 149 says it's God. The psalmist encourages us to rejoice and sing a new song to our awesome God, who made us. He calls us to worship Him with dancing and music. Why? Because "the LORD takes delight in his people; he crowns the humble with victory" (v. 4). God created us,

and He holds the universe together. He delights in us just because we're His beloved children. He designed us, knows us, and invites us to get to know and love Him.

Our loving and living God is our reason for everlasting joy. He invites you to share that joy.

How can you show contagious joy to others?

Dear God, thank you for creating the universe and for creating me!

You can read about our reason for joy in Psalm 149:1–5.

DAY 84

FUELED BY FIRE

If we are thrown into the blazing furnace, the God we serve is able to deliver us. . . . But even if he does not . . . we will not serve your gods.

DANIEL 3:17–18

When two weary firefighters stopped at a restaurant for breakfast, the server recognized the men from the news and realized they'd spent the night battling a fire. To show her appreciation for their courage, she wrote a note on their bill, "Your breakfast is on me today. Thank you . . . for serving others and for running into the places everyone else runs away from."

In the Old Testament, we see courage in the actions of Shadrach, Meshach, and Abednego. These young men courageously showed their love for God by not bowing down to a statue of the king. Their penalty was to be thrown into a blazing furnace. Yet they didn't back down: "If we are thrown into the blazing furnace, the God we serve is able to deliver us from it, and he will deliver us from Your Majesty's hand. But even if he does not . . . we will not serve your gods or worship the image of gold" (Daniel 3:17–18). God *did* rescue them and even walked with them in the fire.

If you're having a difficult time right now, you can know that God is with you. He can help you through.

What fiery trial do you need God to help you through?

Dear God, please give me the courage to face _____.

You can read about Shadrach, Meshach, and Abednego in Daniel 3:13–18, 25–27.

DAY 85

LIGHT FOR THE PATH

How sweet are your words to my taste,
sweeter than honey to my mouth!

PSALM 119:103

On Chicago Day, October 9, 1893, many businesses shut down because the owners thought everyone would be attending the world's fair. Over seven hundred thousand people did! But evangelist Dwight Moody wanted to fill a music hall at the same time on the other end of Chicago with preaching and teaching. His friend R. A. Torrey doubted Moody could draw a crowd that day. But he did. As Torrey later concluded, the crowds came because Moody knew "the one Book that this old world most longs to know—the Bible."

Through Moody's teaching and the Holy Spirit at work, many people came to Christ—and learned to love the Bible—at the end of the nineteenth century in Chicago.

The psalmist exclaimed, "How sweet are your words to my taste, sweeter than honey to my mouth!" (Psalm 119:103).

God's messages of grace and truth acted as a light for the psalmist's path, a lamp for his feet.

Do you read the Bible? As you do, God will increase your love for Him. And if you have questions, you can ask your parents, Sunday school teacher, or other trusted adult for help.

Where do you go if you have
questions about the Bible?

*Dear God, help me to read the Bible
so I can learn to love it too.*

You can read about the psalmist's love
for Scripture in Psalm 119:97–105.

DAY 86

OUR FATHER SINGS

He . . . will rejoice over you with singing.

ZEPHANIAH 3:17

Dandy loves encouraging people by singing to them. One day he was having lunch at his favorite restaurant, and he noticed that the server was having a bad day. He asked her a few questions and then started quietly singing a catchy, upbeat song to cheer her up. "Well, kind sir, you just made my day. Thank you so much," she said with a big smile.

Did you know God loves to sing? The prophet Zephaniah described God as a musician who loves to sing for and with His children. He wrote that God "will take great delight in you; in his love he will no longer rebuke you, but will rejoice over you with singing" (Zephaniah 3:17). God promised always to be with those who love Him. But He also invites and joins in with His people to "be glad and rejoice with all your heart" (v. 14).

One day we'll be together with God and with all those who've put their trust in Jesus as their Savior. Imagine hearing your heavenly Father sing as He welcomes you into His loving arms.

What do you imagine God singing about when He sees you?

Thank you for loving me, God.

You can read about God's love in Zephaniah 3:14–17.

DAY 87

PRINTED ON OUR HEARTS

*Bind them on your fingers; write them
on the tablet of your heart.*

PROVERBS 7:3

When Johannes Gutenberg combined the printing press
with movable type in 1450, the era of mass communication
began. Literacy increased across the globe and new ideas
spread. Because of his invention, Gutenberg produced the
first-ever printed version of the Bible. Before this, Bibles
had to be carefully hand-copied, taking scribes up to a year
to produce a single copy. Can you imagine that?

Ever since that day, the printing press has given us direct
access to Scripture. Now we also have electronic versions,
but we have actual copies of the Bible because of this invention. What was once available only to princes, nobles,
and scholars is now affordable and available for anyone.

Having access to God's truth is an amazing privilege. The
writer of Proverbs says we ought to cherish the words of
the Bible with great fondness and write God's words of

wisdom on "the tablet of [our] heart" (7:3). As you seek to read and understand the Bible, you'll gain wisdom and truth to help you live your life for Him, which is what God wants for you.

Have you learned to cherish the Bible?

Dear God, thank you for the Bible, which helps me to know about you.

You can read about the importance of Scripture in Proverbs 7:1–4.

DAY 88

KNOW HIS VOICE

*I am the good shepherd; I know my sheep
and my sheep know me.*

JOHN 10:14

One year for vacation Bible school, Ken's church decided to bring in live animals. When he arrived to help, Ken was asked to take a sheep inside. He had to practically drag it by a rope into the church gym. But as the week went on, the sheep became less reluctant to follow him. By the end of the week, Ken didn't have to hold the rope anymore; he just called the sheep and it followed, knowing it could trust him.

In the New Testament, Jesus compares himself to a shepherd, saying that His people, the sheep, will follow Him because they know His voice. But those same sheep will run from a stranger or thief. Like sheep, we (believers in Jesus) get to know the voice of our Shepherd through our relationship with Him. And as we do, we see how good He is and learn to trust Him.

As you grow to know and love God, you'll be better able to understand how to live for Him and to run from people who try to trick you and draw you away from God. You can trust the voice of the Shepherd to lead you to safety.

What is one way you can learn more about the Good Shepherd?

Jesus, thank you for taking care of me.

You can read about the Good Shepherd in John 10:1–10.

DAY 89

NO MISUNDERSTANDING

*We know that in all things God works
for the good of those who love him.*

ROMANS 8:28

Alexa, Siri, and other voice assistants can sometimes misunderstand us. A six-year-old talked to her family's new device about cookies and a dollhouse. Later her mom received an email saying an order of seven pounds of cookies and a $170 dollhouse were on their way to her home. Even a talking parrot in London somehow ordered a package of gift boxes. One person asked their device to "turn on the living room lights," and it replied, "There is no pudding room."

God never misunderstands us when we talk with Him, and He's never confused. He knows our hearts better than we do. The Spirit inside us understands God's will and guides us. The apostle Paul told the churches in Rome that God promised to mature us and make us more like

His Son. Even when we don't know what we should ask, the Spirit prays according to God's will for us.

Do you have trouble knowing how to pray? Say what you can from the heart. The Spirit will understand and work out God's good purposes for you.

What do you want God to understand about you?

Dear God, help me to know how to pray.

You can read about how God works for our good in Romans 8:26–30.

MAKING HIS MUSIC

We all . . . are being transformed into his image.

2 CORINTHIANS 3:18

Arianne Abela was born with fingers missing or fused together on both hands. So she grew up sitting on her hands to hide them. In college, that all changed. Arianne planned to major in government. But one day her choir teacher asked her to conduct the choir. Even though it made her hands quite visible, she loved conducting. She'd found her career! She went on to conduct church choirs and then choirs at a university. "My teachers saw something in me," she explains.

Her story invites believers in Jesus to ask: What does God, our holy Teacher, see in us, regardless of our "limits"? God sees himself in us. "So God created human beings in his own image. In the image of God he created them; male and female he created them" (Genesis 1:27 NLT).

As His "image bearers," we were made to reflect Christ. For Arianne, that means Jesus—not her hands or her lack of fingers—matters most. The same is true for all believers. It doesn't matter what we look like. We're "being transformed into his image," says 2 Corinthians 3:18. He helps us, through His Spirit, to grow more and more like Him.

How do you think God is transforming you?

Dear Jesus, help me to be more like you.

You can read about what it means to be transformed in 2 Corinthians 3:17–18.

Spread the Word
by Doing One Thing.

- Give a copy of this book as a gift.

- Share the QR code link via your social media.

- Write a review of this book on your blog, favorite bookseller's website, or at ODB.org/store.

- Recommend this book to your church, small group, or book club.

Connect with us. [f] [○]

Our Daily Bread Publishing
PO Box 3566, Grand Rapids, MI 49501, USA
Email: books@odb.org

GOD HEARS HER

Seek and she will find

get creative

with

your devotional time

GOD
HEARS
You!

Another 90-day devotional for YOU!

Order today

Live BOLDLY

for JESUS!

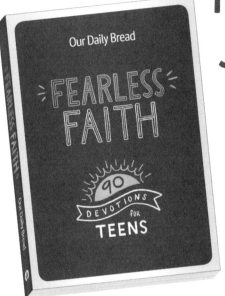

Empower teens to live a bold, courageous, faith-filled life with this engaging 90-day devotional.

Order today